132 Seize the Days

132: Seize the Days
Published January 2007
by Lonely Planet Publications Ltd

Head office:
90 Maribyrnong Street, Footscray, Vic 3011, Australia
Locked Bag 1, Footscray, Vic 3011, Australia

Branches:
150 Linden Street, Oakland CA 94607, USA
72-82 Rosebery Avenue, London EC1R 4RW, UK

ISBN: 978-1-74179-144-0

Text & illustrations © Lonely Planet Publications Ltd 2007

Printing supplied through Breathe Print Management LLP and printed in Spain.

Statistics sources: p8, These statistics were reproduced with permission from Croner, part of Wolters Kluwer (UK) Limited, sidebar – www.employersforwork-lifebalance.org.uk; p9, www.managers.org.uk/news_1.aspx?news= 3:3021&id=3:183&id=3:9, www.prnewswire.co.uk/cgi/news/release?id=114389, sidebar – www.statistics.gov. uk/cci/nugget.asp?id=440; p10, http://news.bbc.co.uk/2/hi/europe/4536891.stm, www.gnn.gov.uk/environ-ment/detail.asp?ReleaseID=43605&NewsAreaID=2&NavigatedFromDepartment=False; p11, www.samaritans.org. uk/know/campaigns/stress/stressresults.pdf, www.jobsite.co.uk/career/advice/health.html, www.onrec.com/con-tent2/news.asp?ID=2103, www.nclnet.org/stress/summary.htm, www.samaritans.org.uk/know/campaigns/stress/ stressresults.pdf; p42, http://news.bbc.co.uk/1/hi/talking_point/2939944.stm, http://news.bbc.co.uk/1/hi/busi-ness/5082070.stm; p43, www.managers.org.uk/print_news_1.aspx?news=3:3021&id=3:183&id=3:9.

contents

^R Where you see this symbol turn to the Resources chapter.

i don't have time

When was the last time you said that? Yesterday? Last week? Or no time to even think about it? It's the excuse for everything from not getting the car serviced to never taking that trip of your dreams, not booking an after-work massage to never learning a language, not surprising your partner with a spontaneous dinner to never quite getting started on that great novel you've almost certainly got in you.

fact: you **DO** have time

add it up

Weekends: 2 days x 52 weeks = **104** days

Bank holidays:
New Year
Good Friday
Easter Monday
May Day
Spring Bank Holiday
August Bank Holiday
Christmas Day
Boxing Day   = **8** days

Statutory annual paid leave: = **20** days

Total   = **132** days

in 132 days or less
here's what's already been done

0.34 days Pemba Dorje Sherpa climbed the south side of Everest, from Base Camp to the summit, in 8 hours and 10 minutes on 21 May 2004 – the fastest ascent of the world's tallest mountain.

7.37 days In May 2006 magician David Blaine remained submerged in a saltwater bubble outside New York's Lincoln Centre for a record 177 hours.

39.83 days In 1991 it took Mohammed Salahuddin Choudhury of Calcutta and his wife Neena 39 days and 20 hours to travel all the way around the globe by car (24,901 road miles) in the fastest time ever.

65 days Bob Timm and John Cook made what remains the longest ever continuous flight in 1959, flying a distance comparable to six times round the world in 65 days without landing even once.

99 days It took Japanese adventurer Mitsuro Ohba 99 days to walk, ski and parasail a total of 2376 miles in the longest ever solo Antarctic walk in 1998.

and here's what you could do

0.13 days Run the London Marathon in three hours.[R]

14 days Circumnavigate the globe by hot air balloon.

21 days Drive the charity Plymouth–Banjul challenge in a car worth less than £100 (p108).

45 days Build an ice hotel with around 60 co-workers.

54 days Cross the Sahara by camel.

90 days Take the annual three-month Buddhist Rains Retreat in Thailand.[R]

100 days Write a novel.[R]

120 days Walk from John O'Groats to Land's End.

132 days Cycle coast to coast across the USA.

[R] Where you see this symbol turn to the Resources chapter.

"**4** out of **5** UK workers don't use their full annual leave entitlement; over **25%** have more than **7 days** holiday left at the end of the year." Croner

top 3 rubbish excuses for not taking leave

:: 'I'm too busy.'
:: 'I've got nothing planned.'
:: 'I can't – who would do my work?'

laptop **on the lilo**

Even though two-thirds of UK managers receive at least five weeks paid leave per year (which is more than ever before) a survey by the Chartered Management Institute showed that when they do finally get away, many just can't stop working.

:: 68% respond to requests from their boss while on holiday
:: 48% check work emails and 43% check their work voicemail
:: 23% worry about the workload they'll return to

o **come all ye workaholics**

The Work Foundation, BT and Management Today magazine found that 37% of men do unscheduled work at Christmas. Around 24% admitted that work meant they neglected their children in some way; 21% missed their child's Christmas play and 22% are too busy to buy presents for their family.

the **letter of the law**

You're not obliged, by law, to work longer than an average 48-hour week. This can be extended by an 'opt-out', which means a signed contract – either permanent or temporary – which states that you agree to work extra hours. If you change your mind about the opt-out, you must give your employer seven days notice, or up to three months if stipulated in the contract. Only one in three working people, according to the Trades Union Conference, knows that this opt-out protection exists, and one in three of those say they were given no choice.[R]

As for leave entitlement, under the existing law employers are able to include the eight UK bank holidays as part of the minimum four-week annual holiday entitlement. From October 2007 this will no longer be possible – bank holidays will be leave days in addition to four weeks paid leave.

europe's workhorse

According to the European Trade Union Federation, UK employees work longer hours than almost all their European contemporaries – an average of 40 hours per week, with one in six workers working over 48. However, this doesn't mean that Britain is the most fruitful country: both France and Germany, with 38.2- and 39.9-hour weeks respectively, outdo Britain in terms of productivity.

Long working hours have become so much part of contemporary culture that there's even a name for an associated – and worrying – condition: 'presenteeism.' A presentee is someone who spends longer hours than necessary at their place of work, simply because they feel it's expected, even if all their day's work has been completed. Shockingly, 81% of British workers say they have experienced this sort of pressure.

country	no of bank holidays
united kingdom	8
germany	9
spain	14
belgium	15
italy	12
france	14

TIME AT WORK | PRODUCTIVITY

gross national happiness

While we in the Western world see the pursuit of happiness as a personal (and sometimes seemingly unattainable) goal, in one country the government has made the good mood of the populace its business. Since 1972 the tiny kingdom of Bhutan has believed its citizens' GNH (Gross National Happiness) says more about quality of life than the usual measurement of GNP. GNH is based on four 'pillars' – environmental preservation, cultural promotion, socio-economic development and good governance. It's yet to be seen whether this means the Bhutanese are a happier people than the Brits.

land of stress & worry

Consistently working long hours and not taking enough holidays is bad for us. It creates stress and health problems, can ruin relationships, causes depression, lowers productivity and makes caring for our children difficult. The proof is in the pudding:

:: A Samaritans survey found that work is the single largest factor causing stress amongst 25 to 44 year olds in Britain.

:: One in five people now suffer from work-related stress, which is now the biggest cause of time off work, even beating the common cold; according to BUPA, 270,000 people take time off because of it every day.

:: 6.7 million working days are lost each year due to decreased productivity as a result of stress.

:: 41% of Britons feel more stressed at work than five years ago.

Have your work-life scales tipped seriously out of balance? Are you leaning precariously, about to tip over into a serious case of burnout?

beware of burnout

what is it?
Burnout is a condition whereby previously motivated, productive people suffer from emotional, physical and mental exhaustion. This can manifest itself in a low sense of personal achievement and a complete (but unsurprising) loss of interest in work.

the signs
Severe stress can cause headaches, teeth grinding, fatigue, digestive problems, psychosomatic illnesses and high blood pressure.

the symptoms
These vary widely, but if you're close to burnout, you might feel powerless, hopeless, drained, frustrated, bored, resentful, irritable, detached from those around you, trapped, uncertain, insecure, cynical and anxious. It's not pretty, but it is avoidable; read on.

> In 1914 the British government abolished Sundays off for the war effort, but productivity fell rather than increased.

reclaim
your free time

step 1
critically assess how you
currently spend your time
go to page 15

step 2
get your head around some
simple rules
go to page 21

step 3
seize the days
from page 25

2007

the
free-time
continuum

And when you do have a breather, do you feel you make the most of it or feel frustrated because 'by the time I finished that work report and had a lie in, the weekend was over'? We work longer hours than in any other part of Europe, which leaves little time to do the washing up let alone pursue our dreams. Read on to discover whether you use your spare time well (if you even give yourself any) and how you can make the most of it again. Think about it: even if you took a lunch hour, that's an extra 10 days a year to yourself...

Crazed workaholic or carefree hedonist? Where do you fit on the Free-Time Continuum? Take our quiz to find out...

1. It's Monday morning and you wake up in:
- O a. A cold sweat
- O b. Ample time
- O c. Amsterdam

2. It's 1pm. You're:
- O a. Skipping lunch. No time to eat
- O b. Eating a sandwich at your desk or seeing clients
- O c. Off to meet friends today, swimming 20 lengths tomorrow. Let voicemail pick up your calls (that's what it's there for)

3. At the end of a working day, you feel:
- O a. Fit for nothing
- O b. Ready to relax on the couch
- O c. Excited. You've got a drinks/dinner/cinema night arranged

4. Do you wake up on a Saturday morning with:
- O a. A conference call
- O b. A carpet to clean
- O c. A coffee and a cuddle

5. What do you think about when you're in the shower?
- O a. The next big project
- O b. Breakfast and what I'm going to wear
- O c. Soap…shampoo…lather…rinse

6. Do you take all your holiday entitlement?
- O a. Never. There is so much work to do
- O b. I try, but sometimes it creeps up on me and I just ask to be paid for the time instead
- O c. Of course. I'm already planning my next trip to Vietnam

7. On your last holiday, you spent:

○ a. Three hours a day in the business centre checking work emails and dealing with important calls

○ b. Three days in Corfu with a last-minute friend on a last-minute package deal

○ c. Three weeks backpacking in Central America (like you've always wanted to)

8. It's your friend's birthday tonight and you haven't bought a present yet. You:

○ a. Are nervous. Time is running out…

○ b. Aren't worried. You've kept your lunch hour free to buy it

○ c. Would never wait until the last minute. You always buy gifts in advance at one of the cool markets you visit on weekends

9. Your boss sets a stressful deadline. You:

○ a. Talk to no one until it's completed

○ b. Take ten-minute breathers for a quick chat with friends

○ c. Plan your time carefully, so you have one night out this week

10. When colleagues ask 'How was your weekend?' you:

○ a. Pretend to have done something exciting when you really spent most of it working

○ b. Usually find something to talk about but think 'is that really all I did all weekend?'

○ c. Admit to that novel you're writing

Now you've answered the questions, what do your answers say about you?

If you picked mostly As...

You're ambitious and things get done at work when you're around, but does it really make you happy? Just taking lunch or getting a decent night's sleep is necessary to recharge your batteries and feel refreshed. Remember: there's nothing wrong with having a personal life or taking time out. If you burn out from working too hard, your performance will suffer. And – sorry – but workaholics can be dull. Having a varied personal life will help you develop wider interests, relax and appear confident.

It's clear you need to spend more time having fun. And your bad habits are well ingrained, so you'll need to **Start Small** (p21).

"Friday evening, I finish late then go for drinks with colleagues. Saturday morning, I struggle out of bed and grab a sandwich en route to the office to get through some extra work while it's quiet. In the evening, I meet my girlfriend and end up criticized about never having time for 'us'. On Sundays, we get up late, have a pub lunch, then I work from home to get a running start on the week ahead."
Chris Dalloway, 38, Corporate Lawyer, Edinburgh

If you picked mostly Bs...

Whether it be a ten-minute window or five hours, you make a conscious effort to fill every spare moment. But – secretly – you think it would be great to stretch yourself more. You want to take a few risks and have fun trying out new things. Endless freedom? So what would you do? If your first thought is a massage, take note, and make room for it each week. And if your week starts to look hectic, a regular 'Thursday drink with Dave' will keep you on track.

> Life is what happens when we're busy making other plans – John Lennon

You're not bad at seizing your days, but you have lots of potential to do more with your free time. Surprise yourself by unleashing a more adventurous you – all you need to do is **Get Out of Your Comfort Zone** (p21).

"5.31pm Friday, I race home to watch Emmerdale and do the washing up, drink some wine, and end up bored and wondering why I didn't plan to go out. Saturday it's chores and a night at the pub with friends who haven't got anything else planned either. Sunday it's more housework, then in the afternoon I'll maybe a see a film or just go for a walk. Then it's Sunday night already and I start to get depressed that it's work again tomorrow."
Amanda Wilson, 28, Landscape Architect, Walsall

If you picked mostly Cs…

Regardless of how hectic or stressed your life can get, you work hard to find the time to pursue other interests. That means looking at your schedule, seeing what you can lose to make time for people and activities that matter the most. Relaxing is essential to staying calm. So you do whatever makes you wind down best, whether it's sports or meeting friends, and ensure you fit these in your life. Your work-life balance is guaranteed if you keep up the good work.

You know what makes you happy and you know how to make the time to get out there and do it. Now all you have to do is make sure you tick off the Big Ones – to do that you'll have to **Think Big** (p21).

"On Fridays I finish work early and meet up with friends to try out a new restaurant or go to an exhibition. Saturday morning I wake late, jog in the park, laze with the paper, then wander to a museum; Saturday nights I usually plan to meet some friends for cocktails. Sunday is market day, and we spend most of the day cooking things we've never tried before, have an enormous dinner and get to bed early for work tomorrow."
Kamal Chaoui, 34, Systems Analyst, London

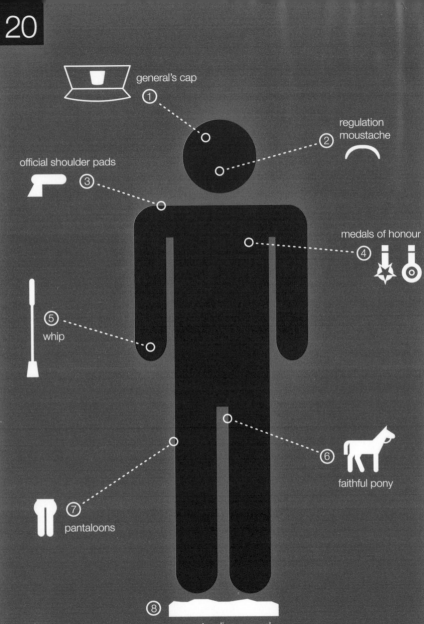

general's cap
1

regulation moustache
2

official shoulder pads
3

medals of honour
4

whip
5

faithful pony
6

pantaloons
7

8
your standing ground

HQ

the
rules of
engage-
ment

start small

(v; sound advice) 1 To embark on a course of exciting, inspiring new actions, one step at a time, in order to enhance life forever. 2 To realise that current ingrained habits are unproductive and take immediate steps to break the routine. 3 To shatter, disperse, disband or terminate a customary, narrow, tedious or uninspiring pattern of thought and replace it with a broad, visionary, lateral and imaginative one.

get out of your comfort zone

querencia (figurative; Spanish) The small area in a bullring to which a bull mysteriously chooses to retreat during a bullfight; a place where it falsely imagines itself to be safe. As the bullfight progresses the adoption of this comfort zone renders the bull predictable and thus causes its eventual downfall. (The moral of the story? Getting out of your comfort zone is a healthy and positive move.)

think big

(v; self-explanatory) 1 To refuse to narrow your perspective or confine your ambitions. 2 To dare to dream in order to reach new heights. 3 To relinquish worry and doubt, realize that there's nothing to lose, and reach for the skies in order to attain happiness and fulfillment.

rule 1:
start
small

rule 2:
get out
of your
comfort
zone

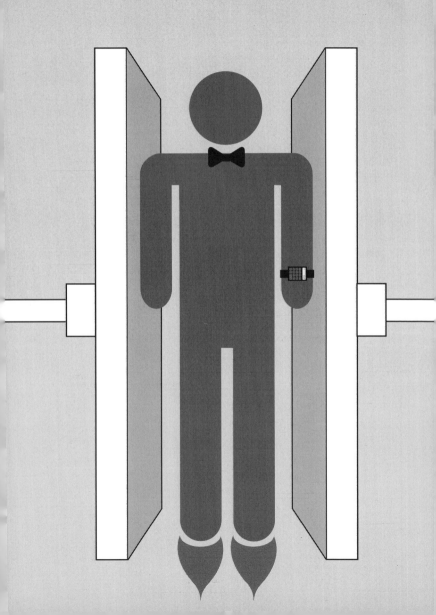

escape

The whole object of travel is not to set foot on foreign land; it is at last to set foot on one's own country as a foreign land
– GK Chesterton

Escape isn't only about travelling to far-flung climes; it's about gaining enough distance to see things afresh. It's easy to forget that while we're plodding through the daily grind, there's a world filled with places, people and endless possibilities going on without us.

bank holiday

There's Gold in Them Thar Streams
Head out into the wilderness to become a prospector with the good ol' boys. With little more than a pan and a pair of galoshes you can try your hand at panning for gold, which is still to be found in British rivers and streams, particularly in Wales, Scotland and the South West.[R]

Art Amongst the Shrubbery
Stroll the sculpture trail for an edifying cultural afternoon in the bracing country air. Across Britain there are dozens of sculpture parks set in parklands, forests and formal gardens.

Reach for the Stars
Buy a telescope and gaze at the moon, or visit an observatory to regain your perspective on the infinite space beyond your office walls. As Oscar Wilde said, we are all in the gutter, but some of us are looking at the stars...

Wander a Windswept Beach
Find the UK's best beaches online where you can search by area, Blue Flag, or Green Coast Awards. If you fall in love with one particular stretch, go one step further and adopt it.[R]

> I did not fully understand the dread term 'terminal illness' until I saw Heathrow for myself – Dennis Potter

Avoid the Bank Holiday Hordes
Childhood bank holidays are a dim memory of endless traffic jams, packed car parks and long waits for the public toilets. But it doesn't have to be that way if you escape the motorway queues and bank holiday hordes. Here are the nation's top five UK Bank Holiday destinations to avoid, together with some less crowded alternatives.

avoid... : try instead...

Edinburgh   **Stirling** – like a mini Edinburgh (complete with hilltop castle), but without the crowds

London   **Bristol** – regenerated docks, Georgian streets, buzzing music scene and loads of great shopping and eating

York   **Durham** – 45 minutes up the trainline from York, Durham has a superb cathedral, a castle you can stay in, and lively student nightlife

Manchester   **Leeds** – comes with Victorian grandeur, endless shopping opportunities, and new bars and clubs springing up all the time

Cambridge   **Norwich** – medieval churches, ancient streets, a castle, a cathedral, a university and some great old pubs

Get Lost
There are mazes all over Britain, from historical hedge-cut labyrinths like Hampton Court maze, created in 1702, to a maze made of maize at St. Bee's.[R]

Take Giant Steps
Motor down the spectacular Causeway Coast in Northern Ireland, following the Antrim Coast Road that passes beneath nine glens, through gorgeous country villages, past the fairytale Dunluce Castle and the famous Giant's Causeway.

Rummage for Rocks
Go fossil hunting on Devon and Dorset's 'Jurassic Coast', a 95-mile stretch of World Heritage coastline where ancient ammonites and belemnites abound.[R]

is it cricket?

In the good old days, contented Victorian bankers acknowledged around 33 religious festivals and saints' days each year. But in 1834 these were pared back to just four bare essentials: May Day, Christmas Day, 1 November and Good Friday.

In 1871 this was set down in the law books by Sir John Lubbock, who adjusted the Bank Holidays Act to accord with what he believed was the most important criteria for holidays: cricket. Lubbock felt strongly that bank managers should have the opportunity to participate in cricket games, so he altered the days to include those on which cricket was traditionally played in the village where he grew up. So, bank holidays became Easter Monday, Whit Monday, the first Monday in August and Boxing Day.

It wasn't until a century later that our current bank holidays (see p5) were instated with the Banking and Financial Dealings Act of 1971, though bank holidays remain subject to yearly royal approval. (So, in theory, if the Queen doesn't feel the need for a Boxing Day holiday we won't get one!)

start small:
top 10 mini escapes

So you're officially terrible at taking time off, or doing anything truly life-enhancing when you do escape. But don't despair – old habits can be broken. It takes 21 days to break a habit or establish a new one, so making a small change every day for the next three weeks will set you well on the way to a new approach to your free time.

1. Listen in at a lunchtime concert.

2. Get a taste of Memento Mori with an atmospheric cemetery stroll through one of Britain's many grand, crumbling Victorian necropoli.[R]

3. Say 'om' at lunchtime meditation. Research shows that 30 minutes' meditation improves your afternoon's productivity.[R]

4. Get cultured at a local museum. Britain has a wealth of lesser-known museums dedicated, amongst other things, to lawnmowers, pencils, forgotten writers, witchcraft and bricks.[R]

5. Reclaim the streets on your lunch hour: explore an area you've never been to before, on foot, or by bike, roller blades or skateboard.

6. Get cooking – many UK cookery schools offer one-hour 'cook your own lunch' lessons.

7. Go hunting for today's equivalent of buried treasure by geocaching – an outdoor treasure-hunting game in which the participants use GPS to hide and seek 'treasure' planted all over the world.[R]

8. Lido lounge '50s-style at one of these great relics: Saltdean Lido in Brighton, Plymouth's Tinside Lido, or Tooting Bec Lido in London.[R]

9. Vamp it up and acquire a provocative new skill by taking a pole- or lap-dancing class, or a burlesque workshop.[R]

10. Take in a film – rent a theatre at your local cinema multiplex, split the cost with a big group of friends and enjoy your favourite film with champagne and Chinese takeaway.

weekend

The Ultimate Lie-In

Take a room in your favourite hotel; empty out the minibar and fill it with gourmet treats, then make like John and Yoko. (If you want the experience to be 100% authentic, head to the Amsterdam Hilton and check into the John and Yoko Suite, unspectacular to look at, but the place where the real bed-in – an anti-war protest – happened in 1969.)

Take an Unusual City Break

Try Fès in Morocco, with one of the largest living medieval cities in the world, or venture to the Egyptian oasis town of Siwa, where beehive-like ruins of the old town are shrouded with date palms. Alternatively, go east to Baku in Azerbaijan, where you can sample caviar from shady dealers in side streets, delve into the ancient caravanserais of the Inner City, and sip vodka overlooking Baku Bay.

Oh I do like to Be Beside the Seaside!

Escape back to your childhood with a good old-fashioned weekend of sticks of rock, Kiss-me-Quick hats, amusement arcades, donkey rides and greasy chips lightly coated in sand. All around Britain and Ireland's coastline are seaside towns with frilly pink B&Bs just waiting to entertain you with a retro Coke Float and a Mr. Punch or two, while you snooze on a stripy deckchair beneath a knotted hankie. Try Blackpool, Southwold or Llandudno for starters.

Disappearing Act

Hide from the world by leaving your mobile phone at home and leaving no clue as to your whereabouts when you escape to a cosy cottage tucked away in the wild, wet wonder of the Lake District, a decommissioned lighthouse on the coast, or a suite fit for a baronet in a remote Highlands castle.

Viva Las Vegas

Escape to the sheer lunacy of it all with a long weekend in Vegas, where you can visit Paris, Venice, New York and the Emerald City in one afternoon, catch a little Barry Manilow in the evening, and make like a lounge lizard in the bar of the Bellagio. If you're in the mood for love, get hitched by an Elvis impersonator at midnight at the Little White Wedding Chapel, or 800ft in the air at the Stratosphere casino's Chapel in the Clouds.

I [heart] NY State

Take a sloop trip on America's mighty Hudson River, or explore the waters of Long Island Sound and Peconic Bay at North Fork, where you'll likely glimpse herons, turtles and hawks along the way.

Ascend to Shopping Nirvana

Yes, Hong Kong has museums, monasteries and Victoria Peak, but hitting the stores is the ultimate shopping experience. Head for chic boutiques for sheer indulgence, or to the multitude of markets for a sensory overload. Hone your bargaining skills at Temple Street Night Market, then peruse the Goldfish Market on Tung Choi Street, or the Bird Market on Yuen Po Street where it's better to browse than buy (since BA understandably isn't keen on stowing songbirds in the overhead compartment).

midweek weekend

If you're trying to avoid planefuls of weekending Brits, you might want to take note of the results of a recent survey of passengers at Stansted Airport. Paris was named top European weekend destination, followed by Rome, Barcelona and Dublin, whilst New York City, then Beijing, were the favourite long-haul weekend destinations. Amsterdam enticed weekend stag partygoers, and Milan was high on the list for shoppers. So slink off midweek to these destinations to allow yourself a little more elbow-room on that bargain basement flight.

week

West Africa by Rail

Take a train journey between Dakar in Senegal and Bamako, the capital of Mali, on what was once one of the most luxurious lines in Africa. Today a shadow of its former glorious self, its crumbling carriages, appalling hygiene and unreliable time-keeping make this a trip for the truly determined escapee; the journey should take 35 hours, but regularly takes three days, leaving you several days at either end to recover by the pool in Dakar or taste the exotic in Bamako.

sleeps **with a twist**

Explore the eccentric side of travel by basing yourself at one of the world's more unusual hotels, where sleep is merely the icing on a weird and wonderful cake.

:: **Sweden** Get to know H_2O with a stay in the underwater Utter Inn in Vasteras where you can watch fish float by from the comfort of your bed – just an hour's drive from Stockholm. Or go for a bigger chill at northern Sweden's seasonal ice hotel, built each year in Jukkasjärvi, 200km north of the Arctic Circle.

:: **Japan** Take your choice – go high-tech or olde-world. Stay at a capsule hotel in Tokyo, where all your material needs are (just) met in a three- by six-foot white plastic hole-in-the-wall. Or head to the village of Awazu, where the Hoshi Ryokan is reputed to be the oldest hotel in the world. It dates back to 717AD when Buddhist monk Taicho Daishi first dreamt of a healing hot springs on the spot.[R]

:: **USA** Taste true eccentricity at the Dog Bark Park Inn in Cottonwood, Idaho, where rooms are situated inside the body of the world's largest beagle. (Yes, you read correctly: beagle.) Then, if your nerves can take it, check into Cassadaga, Florida, a township entirely composed of mystics and seers, where the central motel is, naturally, haunted.

:: **France** Stay in that paragon of '50s travelling style, the Airstream trailer, at a purpose-built campsite in southern France. These metallic bullet-shaped beauties are fully equipped, including minibars.[R]

:: **Turkey** Go underground in Cappadocia at one of dozens of boutique cave hotels with rooms cut deep into the honeycomb-like rock.

:: **Australia** Spend a few nights in the clink at the Old Jail in Mount Gambier where, thankfully, inmate-guests can now lock themselves in and out.

go remote

If distance helps you gain perspective, surely the greater the distance the greater the perspective, right? Escape to the ends of the earth to clear your head.

:: **Foula** This Shetland Island is one of Britain's most remote inhabited islands, with a population of just 30. Marvel at its five soaring peaks and incredible variety of flora and fauna.

:: **Mongolia** In winter attend the Thousand Camel Festival in the remote Gobi Desert; in summer kayak on Lake Hovsgol, said to be the world's most pristine body of fresh water.

:: **Spitsbergen** Wonder at the glory of the aurora borealis on this vast Norwegian island, home to glaciers and polar bears, with a permanent population of less than 3000 people.

:: **Easter Island** Gawp at the monoliths and experience Rapanui island culture at this most remote of destinations, halfway between Tahiti and Chile.

:: **Libya** Explore Leptis Magna, the best Roman remains in the Mediterranean, at this most thrilling of out-of-the-way archaeological sites.

:: **Antarctica** Visit the atmospherically named Deception Island and Paradise Harbor, in the world's most awe-inspiringly remote destination.

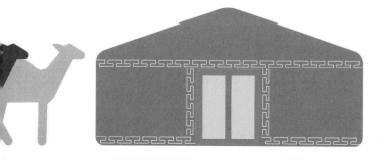

fortnight **or more**

Dream Destinations

Pick out a mythical place that captures your imagination, then escape to find the real thing. Try Timbuktu or Mandalay, Zanzibar or Shangri-la; go in search of the Ark of the Covenant or wander the ruins of Troy.

Island Hop

Explore the crystalline waters of the basin-shaped South Pacific between the great landmasses of America and Asia. Alongside the better-known destinations of Hawaii, Tahiti and Papua New Guinea, there are lesser-discovered neighbours such as miniscule Niue, remote and religious Kiribati, and peculiar Pitcairn, once the final port of call for survivors from the Bounty. Difficult to get to and between, and isolated by miles of open ocean, these are dream destinations for the escapee who wants to leave the cares of the world a million miles away.

Mini Mexico

Shun the Cancun crowds and make for Oaxaca, the artistic capital of Mexico, which is smaller and more tranquil than Mexico City, but every bit as cosmopolitan. Check out the Centro Histórico packed with galleries, Baroque churches such as the Iglesia de Santo Domingo, and savour a local delicacy: chapulines (which are grasshoppers, fried and seasoned with salt, chilli and lime).

Spoil Yourself, Caribbean-Style
If it's a luxury Caribbean escape you're seeking, try one of Barbuda's opulent hidden gems, such as the chic Beach House. A sprinkling of decent B&Bs mean it's also accessible if your wallet's not quite so well padded.

America's North to South
Drive the longest motorable road in the world. The Pan-American Highway, which runs from Deadhorse, Alaska, to Puerto Montt in Chile, means over 16,000 miles behind the wheel, though between Panama and Colombia you'll have to ferry-hop around what's known as the Darien Gap, a lush, impassable area of rainforest.

Ply the Silk Route
Journey from bleak Turkmenistan, through desolate deserts to Uzbekistan's Samarkand, and then on to Tashkent. If you've time aplenty, you can then plough on through little-visited Kyrgyzstan and into China, taking a worthwhile diversion south on the Karakorum Highway. Next, head east through the Taklamakan desert and south on ancient Silk Route trails of Xinjiang province, across the soaring Tibetan Plateau to Llasa and on through dizzying Himalayan heights to Nepal's colourful Kathmandu.

offsetting your jetsetting

One single short-haul flight produces as much CO_2 gas as three months driving a 1.4 litre car. Visit www.lonelyplanet.com/climatecare to calculate and offset your carbon emissions. It's easy and surprisingly cheap!

think big:
cairo to cape town

7 days

This exotic trip begins in the shadow of the ancient Pyramids at Giza or Saqqara, best seen at sunrise on horseback from the edge of the shifting desert sands. A one-week whistle-stop adventure will then whisk you south by Wagonslit sleeper train to the bleak majesty of the Valley of the Kings at palm-studded Luxor and on to languid Aswan with its mighty dam, before hightailing it back to delve headlong into the sights, sounds and smells of teeming, tumultuous Cairo.

30 days

For precarious passage along unpaved roads and nights of desert camping beneath the stars, press on from Aswan by ferry across the immense Lake Nasser to Wadi Halfa in Sudan, through the Nubian desert to Khartoum, then past the incredible Blue Nile Falls to Addis Ababa in Ethiopia. Head south to the magnificent game parks of Kenya, through acacia-filled savannah to Tanzania and the Serengeti. From there, catch the ferry to mythical, magical Zanzibar to soak up the sun on its laid-back beaches before heading for home from Dar-es-Salaam.

132 days

Head from Zanzibar to Malawi, skirting its immense lake, and through once war-torn Mozambique to Zimbabwe and the mile-wide Victoria Falls. On to Botswana and the Kalahari, to Namibia and the desolate Skeleton Coast, and end with a good bottle or two of South African Merlot in swish Cape Town. With endless stop offs, variations and diversions en route your adventure through the heart of Africa can easily fill 132 days, with enough left undiscovered to warrant endless return trips.

> As long as you're thinking at all, you might as well think big – Donald Trump

start small:
how to pull a convincing sickie

Up to one third of British workers are happy to take fake sick days off work, primarily due to hangovers, good weather or birthdays. Unofficial absences cost UK companies as much as £11.6 billion per year, and most employers think that about 30% of sick days taken are fake.

So how do you pull off a convincing sickie? Well, according to public sector union Amicus, it's quite difficult for an employer to prove that you're not really sick if it's just one day off – even if they don't believe there's anything wrong with you – so it seems you've just got to be careful about how you do it.

GET PRE-SICK IN ADVANCE Demonstrate a few symptoms the day before you intend to be off work: the odd cough, a box of tissues on your desk, popping out to the chemist at lunchtime, looking quietly wan and worn-out – but make it subtle. Moaning too much about how ill you feel all day is sure to rouse suspicion with your workmates (who will no doubt recognise your ploy, having used it themselves on occasion).

PREPARE YOUR CALL-IN Consider who you'll have to deal with when you make The Call, and adjust the time of your call accordingly to make sure you speak to the most gullible and sympathetic manager or, best of all, their voicemail. Have your simple, foolproof, health-related excuse prepared, along with answers to tricky questions such as "Will you be in tomorrow?" (the correct answer is "I don't know, but I hope so").

MAKE SURE YOU DON'T GET CAUGHT The damage will be irreparable if you bump into your boss out on an impromptu lunchtime shopping trip.

DON'T DO IT TOO OFTEN Remember the story of the boy who cried wolf: too many sickies will mean a total lack of sympathy and a high level of suspicion when you're finally genuinely ill.

think big:
how to negotiate a month off work

It might seem impossible, but with some compelling arguments you can persuade your boss that an extended period of time off would be beneficial for both you and your company.

FOCUS ON THE BOTTOM LINE Point out your potential increased productivity upon your return; 87% of UK managers agree that taking time off to recharge corporate batteries helps to ensure that the companies function to optimum productivity levels.

SOLEMNLY SWEAR Promise to take the extra time off in lieu of reading the news, sending non-work related emails and buying online during working hours. (The average UK employee spends an estimated 14 working days per year doing non-work-related activities at work.)

ACCENTUATE THE POSITIVES Put the case to your employer by explaining the valuable skills you'll gain from time off: a new language, leadership experience, problem-solving and tackling challenges, adaptability and negotiation skills.

SETTLE BACK IN Finally, explain that, with your itchy feet scratched by life on the road, you'll be more settled, committed and focussed on work when you get back from your adventure.

BACK-UP PLAN If all else fails, save up and offer to take the month off unpaid.

reflect

If we could see the miracle of a single
flower clearly, our whole life would change
– Buddha

Each of the world's religions has its own built-in mechanism
for forcing people to stop what they're doing and simply reflect on the bigger picture. But for many of us, these moments
have been lost in the rush of modern life. From alarm clock
to nightcap, we're dashing from one thing to another, filling
every second with relentless activity. But everyone's inner life
needs a little nurturing now and then.

1.

2.

3.

4.

5.

6.

bank holiday

Hills, Dales, Glades & Brooks
Get lost in Britain's most ancient woodlands and forests. The Woodland Trust has a searchable woods directory, so you can find a tranquil wooded glade near you.[R]

It's a Riot
Laugh your troubles away at a Laughter Club, where the laughs are forced out until they become real – it's fake-it-till-you-make-it and it works. Made popular by Indian doctor Madan Kataria, there are now over 5000 laughter clubs worldwide where participants engage in fits of giggles, titters, chortles and guffaws.[R]

Hug Some Sacred Stones
Avebury is an ancient megalithic monument site and an alternative to the tourist trap at Stonehenge. Sacred stone sites abound in Britain – seek out more mystical energy centres online.[R]

Take the Plunge
Go for a swim somewhere natural. Try a swimming pond, river, lake, or head for the sea. Visit the Outdoor Swimming Society online for tips on when and where to swim in the UK.[R]

Relaxation, Chinese-Style
Try out T'ai Chi, the ancient martial art you'll see practised to perfection in parks across China. Combining slow-motion routines with meditation, it's said to bring about an inner calmness.[R]

Mystic Meditation
Try a crash course in Mystic Rose meditation. Although it seems more than a little strange, old hands swear by the healing power of this meditation technique. Divided into three sections, you'll spend part of the time laughing, part crying, and the other part – known as 'the Watcher on the Hill' – simply reflecting in silence.

Dear Diary...
Buy a weighty-looking journal and reflect on your life by starting a diary. Writing regularly will keep your creative juices flowing, and words on a page will bring back memories – both happy and helpful – later on.

Float It Out
Let your cares float away in a floatation tank, a warm, dark tank of salt-rich water, guaranteed to calm the soul (unless you're highly claustrophobic).

Botanical Remedies
Revive your senses at a tranquil botanical garden. Some, like the Chelsea Physic Garden and the National Botanic Garden of Wales' Apothecaries Garden, were founded specifically to promote the study of botany in relation to medicine and are plentiful with medicinal plants and herbs. Others, with quiet corners, hothouses and woodland glades, make perfect places to simply stroll and smell the daisies.

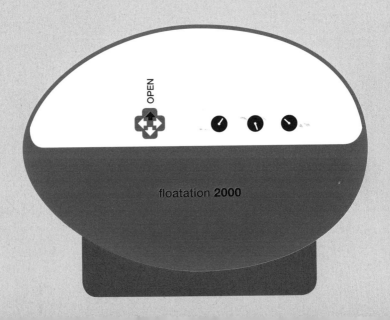

weekend

Open Your Mind
Take a Basic Buddhism weekend course at the tranquil Tara Buddhist Centre, set in an old Derbyshire stately home. Think about the nature of the mind, life and death, stroll in the peaceful grounds and contemplate the universe over a cappuccino at the World Peace Café.[R]

Blessed Be the Silent
Relax into a weekend of quiet reflection on Caldey Island in Pembrokeshire, a holy island populated by Cistercian monks who observe silence between 7pm and 7am, and rise at 3.15 every morning. They're happy to receive contemplative visitors at St. Philomena's retreat house.[R]

Monolithic Reflections
Spend a Greek weekend exploring the atmospheric abandoned monasteries of Meteora, on the Plain of Thessaly, around 200 miles from Athens. Base yourself in the quiet town of Kalambaka, from which all 24 Byzantine buildings, perched incredibly on top of massive rocky monoliths, are a several-mile hike uphill on steps hewn into the rock face. (Bear in mind that ancient pilgrims weren't availed of this convenience and had to be hauled up to the top in baskets.)

> A poor life this if, full of care, we have no time to stand and stare – WH Davies

Creative Study

Get out into the countryside with your camera or sketchbook for a weekend's photography or painting course. At picturesque Kirkudbright in southwest Scotland, for example, you can take a one- or two-day crash photography course with professional guidance that will quickly get you reflecting on the wonderful world around you.[R]

Limber Body; Mind to Follow

Head to Cornwall for a yoga weekend: two days of stretching and breathing your cares away amid a soothing sea breeze.[R]

Sober Reflection

Reflect on the course of modern history at the Intercontinental Berchtesgaden Resort spa in the Bavarian Alps. Now a luxury destination offering glorious pampering, this was once the site of Nazi Reich Marshall Hermann Goring's rural retreat, where Hitler, Goebbels and Goering plotted their monstrous acts of WWII. After a morning floating in the hotel pool, you can visit Kehlsteinhaus, known as Hitler's 'Eagle's Nest', in an odd juxtaposition of relaxed and sombre contemplation.

> All man's miseries derive from not being able to sit quietly in a room alone – Blaise Pascal

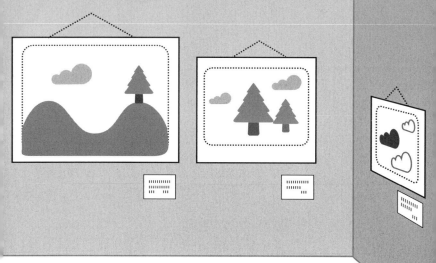

the art of **SHUTTING UP**

*When from our better selves we have too long
Been parted by the hurrying world, and droop,
Sick of its business, of its pleasures tired,
How gracious, how benign, is Solitude.*
– William Wordsworth

When was the last time you said, heard or thought nothing for more than a few seconds? We're constantly being assaulted by noise – mobile phones, radios, sirens, inane TV babble, even the constant chatter of our inner voice. More and more people are turning to silence as a way to switch off from the incessant buzz of modern life, with silent retreats of all types and creeds – Buddhist, Christian, Tao, Zen and more – springing up all over Britain. Keep Mum in a convent or monastery, or take a course in Primordial Sound Meditation to soothe your ragged nerves and reflect on what's really important in life.[R]

week

Purge Your Psyche

If you're feeling brave – and flush – consider an eight-day high-powered retreat to reflect on your past, present and future with the trendy Hoffman Process, an intensive course to help resolve issues relating to self-esteem and relationships.[R]

Work for Your (Luxury) Supper

Join a Willing Hands Week at the White Mountain Retreat in Crete where, in exchange for working on gardening and landscaping projects, you can make use of the fantastic retreat facilities overlooking a serene Mediterranean bay.[R]

Rewire Your Mind

Remember TV hypnotist Paul McKenna? Well, he's just one of the many devotees of NLP, neuro-linguistic programming, which he claims can radically change your life by changing the way you think about yourself in just seven days. Sign up for a week-long course to find out whether the hype is justified.[R]

get out of your comfort zone: el camino de santiago

The earth is criss-crossed with pilgrimage trails, walked since antiquity by people in search of spiritual fulfilment or as an act of religious devotion. One of the most famous still-walked routes in the world is El Camino de Santiago, or the Way of St James, which takes pilgrims to the Spanish cathedral Santiago de Compostela where the apostle St James is said to be buried. The most popular route to the cathedral is the French Way, beginning in either Le Puy, Arles, Tours, or Vezelay, and heading up over the mighty Pyrenees into Spain.

The entire walk takes around four weeks to complete, but with just a week to spare it's possible to complete the final 100km section of the route, staying in simple pilgrims' hostels along the way. When you arrive in Santiago to pick up your Compostela certificate from the Pilgrim's Office to mark your achievement, your name will be read out to the congregation of the noontime Pilgrim's Mass.

nature's lavish show

Head to a natural wonder to reflect on the extraordinary nature of the universe.

:: **Wadi Rum** (Jordan) Lose yourself in the shifting dunes and deafening silences of this incredible, shimmering stretch of desert.

:: **Iguaçu Falls** (Argentina and Brazil) Rivalled only by southern Africa's Victoria Falls and Venezuela's Angel Falls, these roaring torrents stretch for 3km through gorgeous rainforest and encompass the Garganta de Diablo, or Devil's Throat, the world's mightiest single waterfall.

:: **Ngorongoro Crater** (Tanzania) Tens of thousands of wild animals roam the basin-shaped plains created by an ancient volcano.

:: **Great Barrier Reef** (Australia) Reflect beneath the waves along the incredible, enchanting 2000km underwater archipelago.

:: **Galapagos Islands** (Ecuador) The incredible flora and fauna of these islands spurred Darwin to develop his theory of evolution. Some of the world's most incredible flora and fauna can still be found here.

:: **Parícutin Volcano** (Mexico) This spectacular volcano is said to have erupted out of a cornfield in the 1940s, swallowing two villages in its wake.

:: **Yellowstone National Park** (USA) Home to Old Faithful itself, alongside hundreds of other regularly erupting geysers.

:: **Khumbu Glacier** (Nepal) Stretching from Mount Everest down towards the Nepalese plains, this towering expanse of ice and rock is enough to send shivers down your spine.

:: **Uluru** (Australia) Gaze at the sacred, iconic red rock in the middle of nowhere, the second largest freestanding natural monolith in the world.

:: **Grand Canyon** (USA) Sure, it's a cliché, but if the scope and scale of the Grand Canyon doesn't get you reflecting on the nature of nature itself, then nothing will.

fortnight or more

Thai-Style Reflection
Detox in Thailand at the luxurious Chiva-Som or, for something a little more
rustic, take a boat to The Sanctuary on Ko Pha Nagn and try out the refreshing
herbal steam room, early-morning yoga and incredible vegetarian food.[R]

Shiny Happy People
Visit Vanuatu – an archipelago of 83 islands in the Pacific – to reflect on the art
of happiness. According to a study done by the New Economics Foundation,
residents of Vanuatu are the happiest on the planet, ranking first place in a
'Happy Planet Index'. With perpetual sunshine and paradise beaches, it isn't hard
for the visitor to imagine why, especially since the UK limps into the index at a
miserable 108th place.

A Wholer, Calmer You
Venture Down Under to reflect far away from the cares of your everyday life
at one of Queensland's ecovillages. Stay at Crystal Waters ecovillage, a vision
of sustainable living and tranquillity, where you can unwind in peace and get
holistic therapy treatments.

Peace in the Desert
Unwind at San Pedro de Atacama in Chile, situated in the magical high desert at
the foot of the huge Licancabur volcano, one of the tallest in the Andes. Visit the
Valley of the Moon, once a lakebed, whose salt crystals light up on full moons,
the desolate Valle de la Muerte, and the driest place on earth, the Atacama
Desert, where it hasn't rained for several hundred years.

Hallelujah!
Reflect on the stranger face of religion with a trip to Bible Belt, USA. Tour the
11-acre Cross Garden in Prattsville, Alabama, where hundreds of crudely painted
messages warn of eternal damnation. At the Ave Maria Grotto in Cullman,
Alabama, you can view a miniature Jerusalem and St. Peter's Cathedral, and
check out the World's Largest Ten Commandments in Murphy, North Carolina.
If that's not enough, head either for bizarre Holy Land USA in the Blue Ridge
Mountains of Virginia, or the Holy Land Experience in Orlando, where you can
thrill to a live musical version of the story of Moses.

The Land of 330 Million Gods
Spend a couple of weeks in India, a place sure to awaken the spiritual in you. Go
to Varanasi, that holiest of Hindu places, follow in the Beatles' footsteps and stay
at an ashram in Rishikesh, travel to the Mahabodhi Temple in Bodhgaya where
the Buddha achieved enlightenment, or visit the glorious Golden Temple at
Amritsar, the holiest of Sikh shrines.

Sacred Pursuits
If you've more time to spare, try a one-year course run by the Sacred Trust. You
can learn the secrets of Shamanism or Animal Spirit Medicine. For a shorter
encounter, take a Darkness Visible course, in which you spend several days
blindfolded, in order to calm the mind and see the world anew when you
re-emerge as a sighted person.[R]

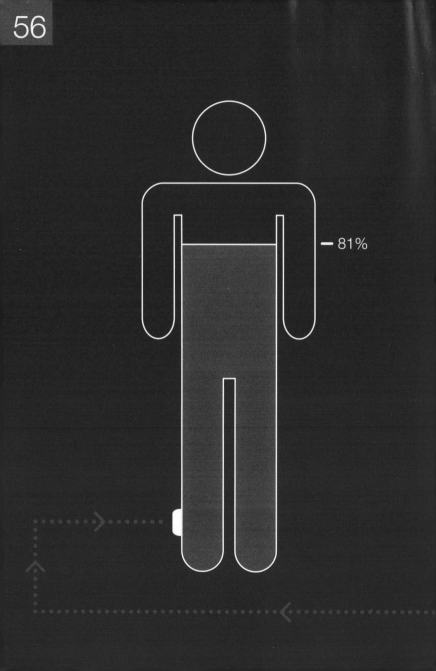

81%

recharge

Those who think they have no time for exercise will sooner or later have to find time for illness
– Edward Stanley

Now you've licked your mind into shape, it's time to get your body moving and recharge your batteries. You can experience adrenaline-pumping adventure close to home, or you can pack your bags and seek your thrills abroad. Either way, when you have to focus on surviving a desert trek, pulling yourself up a steep escarpment or keeping upright on a snowboard, who's got time to worry about work?

bank holiday

Go Ape

Spend an afternoon swinging, scrambling and climbing your way across a challenging course high up in the woodland canopy. There are seven centres in forests across Britain.[R]

Try River Bugging

Become a 'bugger', as you'll affectionately be known, by placing yourself in what looks like an inflatable armchair and hurtling down a stretch of churning white water in this new adrenalin sport direct from the rivers of New Zealand.[R]

A Risk-Free Plunge

Experience the thrill of skydiving, without having to hurl yourself from a tiny plane at 20,000 feet, with a session in a vertical wind tunnel where blasts of 150mph will suspend you in a safe hover above a padded mat.[R]

Get piste

You can ski or snowboard all year round at over 70 dry slopes and snowdomes across the country without leaving Britain. In winter months, head to the Nevis Range or the Cairngorms in Scotland to try telemark or alpine skiing on the genuine white stuff.[R]

Extreme Cycling

Try one of the UK's tough, exhilarating all-weather mountain bike trails; the Forestry Commission's website will help you find a trail that suits you. To seek out sheer drops from which to fling yourself and your two-wheeled steed, tick the 'Severe' box.[R]

Full-Tilt Adventure

For the ultimate adrenaline rush try coasteering, an intense combination of sea swimming, cliff jumping and clambering around rock faces. It's one of the fastest-growing adventure activities across Britain and there are seaside centres across the country.

Climb the Walls

Clamber about on a rock face, either at one of the UK's hundreds of climbing walls or venture outside for the real thing. If you really get a taste for scaling the heights, get on the phone to your local council's planning permission department, then buy the equipment online to build your very own.[R]

Have a Ball

Hurtle down a hillside with sphereing and aquasphering – also known as zorbing – two odd adrenaline activities in which you're either harnessed into a large inflatable bubble-like ball or placed inside along with 30 litres of water and left to career away down steep slopes at speeds of up to 30mph.[R]

week**end**

Go Fly a Kite

Take a weekend course in kite surfing or kite landboarding, where you'll be pulled over water or earth by an oversized kite at exhilarating speeds.[R]

Roll Over History

Take a lengthy, leisurely cycle along Hadrian's Wall on the newly opened Hadrian's Cycleway that follows the path of the wall from the Cumbrian Coast to the North Sea, or walk the Roman Ring, a walking route that promotes sustainable tourism, reducing wear and tear to the historic wall site itself.

Hit the Waves

Get out onto the water and learn how to sail. The Royal Yachting Association lists over a thousand sailing clubs and training centres where you'll be telling your port from your starboard in no time.[R]

alpacas in action

Once upon a time, the only people interested in llamas were the Incas. Nowadays, though, it's not uncommon to see these surprisingly sociable creatures wandering around the countryside of north Yorkshire, Surrey or the Lake District.

There are over half a dozen llama trekking centres in Britain, offering everything from strolls through gentle terrain to several-day hikes through the wilderness for the committed llama-lover. Unlike pony trekking, you don't usually actually ride the llama; rather, it walks along beside you as a trusty companion, carrying your bags or, if you're heading out overnight, your camping equipment.

And if you're in need of fortification along the route, it should be noted that many of Britain's llama trekking centres offer boozy champagne breakfast and pub lunch treks, after which you'll be glad of a four-legged friend to guide you safely home.[R]

Wet 'n' Wild Weekends

Go gorge walking in the Brecon Beacons or canyoning in Scotland. Both involve climbing waterfalls, swimming rapids, jumping gorges and traversing rock faces. Levels of experience and confidence range from complete beginner to complete lunatic.

Attempt the Three Peaks Challenge

Although, officially, this clambering-up of Scafell Pike, Snowdon and Ben Nevis – the highest mountains in England, Wales and Scotland – is supposed to be completed in 24 hours, allow yourself a weekend to get there, get back and recover.

get out of your comfort zone: adrenaline unlimited

Adventure ain't what it used to be. Just a couple of centuries ago, even a simple journey of a few miles could be hazardous, with highwaymen, poor road conditions, temperamental horses and sweeping epidemics to contend with. But today we're travelling more safely than ever before and there are few unexplored corners left on earth.

Perhaps this helps to explain the rise of adrenalin sports. Whether it's zap-catting (hair-raising rides on high powered catamarans), hydrospeeding (solo white-water body rafting), bridge swinging, or rap running (a particularly precarious form of abseiling), more and more Britons are out looking for the ultimate rush, pushing the limits in search of new, extreme thrills. The only limit is your imagination (and your health insurance).

active family fun

Drag the kids away from their computers and video games and get them into action – fun, and good exercise to boot.

:: **Splash** about in the waves with a **boogie-boarding** weekend; lessons for the novice are available (for children and adults alike) at a number of centres around the UK coastline.

:: **Take** to Britain's inland lakes and canals for a weekend of serene **kayaking** with kids, or set out to build a raft and attempt to sail it on shallower shores.

:: **Bond** with the younger generation at a weekend **Outward Bound Family Fun course** in a tradition that dates back to the 1940s. Residential courses last two days, and take place in Wales, Cumbria and Scotland.

:: **Spend** a weekend in the saddle. The west coast of Ireland is a scenic location for **pony trekking** or cantering with the kids, with fantastic luxury B&Bs for the adults amongst you to kick back in the evening.

:: **Try** it all out at one of the Youth Hostel Association's **family mini-breaks**. They offer a host of activities for adults and kids, including abseiling, archery and caving.

week

Turkish Ascent

Hike a section of southern Turkey's spectacular 500km long Lycian Way, which runs from Fethiye to Antalya. The route is easier at the Fethiye end, tougher-going towards Antalya, and takes in a whole host of gorgeous sea views, ruined Lycian cities, expansive beaches and stunning valleys.

India by Camel

Camel trek across the sparse, sometimes eerie Thar Desert, between India and Pakistan. Start and end at the incredible 'Golden City' of Jaisalmer, where tiny sandstone hotels and medieval charm will help you soak up the sun and rest your tender seat after a sore few days in the saddle.

Gliding with the fish

Spend a week in Sardinia or on the Red Sea learning the art of apnea, or free-diving – diving without oxygen tanks. Take a week-long course with Umberto Pelizzari, world record-holding free diver, finding out how to transport yourself to the world beneath the waves with just a lungful of air.

Volcanoes & Vampires

Spend a week riding lively Andalucian horses through the villages and around the volcanoes of Spanish Catalonia, across the mountains and meadows of mid-Portugal, or, for something more offbeat, discovering Dracula's country, along the trails of Transylvania.

Snow Breaks with a Difference

Take an unusual ski break in Cyprus; hit the slopes of Mount Olympos, the highest mountain in the Troodos Mountain range, between January and March, then explore the rest of Cyprus's outdoor treasure, with hikes, bracing swims and rambles around ruins. For something even more exotic, go snowboarding in Lebanon, which has excellent, world-class facilities and slopes at its six resorts, catering to everyone from novice to black-run fanatic, and from budget travellers to seekers of extreme luxury.

> 44% of 18 to 24 year olds are planning a sporty break this year; 19% of over-65s also intend to get active on holiday.

a right royal adventure

Slicing your way along El Camino Real (The Royal Way) – a 40-mile, five-day Panamanian trek, and once the most important route on the Spanish Main – might be the closest you can get in the modern world to true exploration. Originally running from Panama Viejo on the Pacific to the port of Nombre de Dios in the Caribbean, it was, in the 16th century, a two-lane causeway through some of the world's densest jungle, a passageway for plundered Peruvian treasures on their way to Spain. But, abandoned for over a century, the route itself has disappeared, and the trail can now be undertaken with the help of a machete and a head for heights.

The modern-day trek begins in the Chagres National Park, 20 miles outside Panama City, and ends at the sleepy but evocative Portobelo, a Unesco-rated World Heritage site, home to the Black Christ and crumbling ruined forts. With tales of lost bounties, and bounteous jungle life abounding, this journey through the dark heart of Panama – as yet untouched by the tourist trail – is one to set your heart aflutter and your imagination afire.

fortnight **or more**

Take the High Road

Complete the tough, exhilarating 11-day Haute Route from Chamonix to Zermatt, demanding up to eight hours walking per day and nights in mountain huts, and top it off, quite literally, with a three-day ascent of Mont Blanc.

From Sea to Sky

Combine a spectacular road trip with a Rocky Mountain high by taking the grand Canadian Highway 99 – otherwise known as the Sea to Sky Highway – from Vancouver, along the Howe Sound shoreline past stunning lake and mountain scenery, to Whistler, where there's top-notch skiing in winter and adventure sports, mountain biking and golfing in summer.

Survivor!

Take a 16-day jungle survival course in deepest Guyana, hundreds of miles into the rainforest. Complete with former British army instructor, native guides and insect eating, you'll learn how to beat the elements. The last two days are spent with just one companion, fending for yourselves in the wilds.[R]

Outback Adventure

Rent a 4WD and head off to Western Australia's Kimberleys, where you can bump and grind the 600km-long Gibb River Road, a dirt track that takes you past waterfalls, through gorges and along steep escarpments. Alternatively, let someone else do the hard work by buying a Gibb River bus pass, which allows you unlimited stops to sip champagne, view ancient rock art, hike and swim along the way.[R]

get out of your comfort zone: 20,000 leagues under the sea

Perhaps the ultimate adventure for the intrepid – and super-solvent – recharger is a place on the first ever submersible dive at 90 degrees north. Scheduled for August 2008, this is a £55,000, 17-day journey to a place no-one has seen before: 4,400 metres beneath the Arctic Ocean. Setting off by icebreaker from Spitsbergen, you'd be dropped off at the North Pole and transferred to a MIR submersible, a mini-submarine, in which you'll be transported to the freezing depths. No one yet knows what you might find, though scientists predict that it'll be mostly barren, with a few bottom-dwelling creatures here and there. Nevertheless, you'd return home with an interesting conversation piece for your next dinner party, and a murky picture or two for that after-dinner slide show.[R]

camp it up

Camping can be as rough or as gentle as you like, but it's always a great way to recharge drained batteries. Take your sleeping bag or twelve-tog duvet, a kettle or a cafetiere, and venture out for a stint in the wilderness, at home or abroad.

: : **Gavarnie** (French Pyrenees) Within sight of the natural wonder that Victor Hugo called 'nature's amphitheatre', try La Bergerie, a simple, budget campsite with some of the best tent-side mountain views you could hope for. Alternatively, bed down in a 'tipi' at Tipis Indiens.[R]

: : **Angel Island** (San Francisco Bay) A stone's throw from the big city itself, but a world away in peace and tranquility, this pristine island offers a number of basic camping options amid gorgeous island scenery.[R]

: : **Pembrokeshire Coast National Park** (Wales) Rent a yurt or bring your own shelter to Trellyn campsite, a wooded valley less than 100 yards from lovely Abercastle beach.[R]

: : **Blackberry Wood** (East Sussex) Perfect for exploring the South Downs Way and not far from Brighton, Blackberry Wood is set in beautiful woodland, a haven of tranquility for happy campers.

: : **Cottar's 1920 Safari Camp** (Masai Mara) For the ultimate in luxury camping, travel back in time to the grand old days of camping at Cottar's. Tents are furnished with antiques and come equipped with private dressing rooms.[R]

party

If you never did you should. These things are fun and fun is good.
– Dr Seuss

While it's undoubtedly beneficial to feel pure and healthy in mind and body, often what makes us happiest is having an old-fashioned good time. Hedonists – for whom fun is an end to itself and a raison d'etre – are often viewed with disapproval, but it's the kind of disapproval behind which lurks a shade of envy. A little hedonism – as long as it doesn't involve too many late nights or dubious toxins – can be just what the doctor ordered. And there are no better days to seize than the ones that have been marked especially for partying.

spring

Go Wild in the 'Dam

Spend a wild weekend in Amsterdam, celebrating the Queen's birthday with Koninginnendag on 30 April. It's all about raucous drinking and drunken dancing on back-to-back barges on the Prinsengracht, Herengracht and Keizersgracht canals. In order to blend with the locals you'll need to dress entirely in orange, preferably with an extremely silly hat, and be constantly clutching a large glass of lukewarm Heineken. The night before, revel in parties at clubs, bars and cafés across town until the small hours.

Start the Chinese New Year with a Bang

Celebrate Chinese New Year in all its colourful, noisy glory. Taking its exact dates from the Chinese lunar calendar, this 15-day party culminates in the dazzling Lantern Festival. Chinese New Year festivities held in London and San Francisco, with two of the best-known Chinatowns outside Asia, are well worth attending for their fireworks and mouth-watering food. Don't, however, buy a pair of shoes or get a haircut in between the feasts and firecrackers; both are considered inauspicious throughout the festival period.

of buns & nuts, pies & parsons

Some of Britain's quirkiest events take place at Easter, when traditions dating back hundreds of years are kept alive and well. On Good Friday, The Widow's Son Tavern in Bromley-by-Bow hosts a '**bun ceremony**', where a sailor adds an annual bun to the 200-year-old collection in memory of a widow whose son never came back from sea. Easter Saturday in Bacup, Lancashire, sees the appropriately-named **Nutters Dance**, a bizarre form of Morris Dancing.

Perhaps, though, the oddest traditions can be witnessed on Easter Monday in Hallaton, Leicestershire. First, there's the **Hare Pie Scramble**, which involves the vicar flinging handfuls of a huge hare pie into the hungry crowd, followed by the often bloodthirsty **Bottle-kicking Contest** in which two teams fight over three casks of beer – with neither a bottle nor a kick in sight. In 1790 the local rector tried to ban these events because of their pagan origins, but graffiti soon appeared on the vicarage wall proclaiming "No pie, no parson". If you can't beat 'em, join 'em, thought the church – and so it did.

Paint the Town Holy

Join the tumultuous crowds at Varanasi, the holy Indian city sprawled along the banks of the Ganges, to celebrate Holi. This festival of colour is held every year around March to mark the coming of Spring and celebrate the death of Holika, the demon of winter. Tonnes of coloured tika powder are flung at anything that moves, and bonfires and dancing fill Varanasi's ancient lanes and passageways all through the night. It's loud, frenetic, messy and unmissable.

One for Folk Folk

Cheltenham Folk Festival in late February, which has been running for over a decade, was praised by Andy Kershaw as offering "all that is strong and admirable and exciting about British folk music". A cheerful way to liven up a gloomy February weekend, you could also consider volunteering backstage to see the friendly festival from the inside out.[R]

Celebrate with the Celebs

Be dazzled by the flashing of paparazzi bulbs along the Croisette at May's Cannes Film Festival, where you can rub shoulders with the rich and famous, attend grand movie premieres and sip champagne at the water's edge. Bring your best party clothes and your best blagging abilities.[R]

> In our leisure, we reveal what kind of people we are – Ovid

Fire Up
Experience April's Beltane Fire Festival in Edinburgh, where 15,000 people turn out to this pagan celebration of fire that marks the end of winter and the rebirth of spring. The spectacular rituals involve lots of fire, drumming, body paint and sexual innuendo (well, it's a fertility rite, after all). Sparklers compulsory.[R]

24hr Party People
Lose yourself in rhythm at the Winter Music Conference, held annually in March in Miami. It's the best dance music event – with the biggest name DJs – on the planet, where you can revel 24/7 along with tens of thousands of partygoers at some of the coolest clubs in the USA.[R]

summer

Hippy Revelry

Europe's biggest green festival is the splendid Big Green Gathering in August in Somerset, where you can have your fill of tipis, chakras and shamans. If it's your cup of herbal tea, you can also become a steward, for which you'll be fed, watered and put up for free in return for four or five shifts.

Poached Puffin Anyone?

Go remote to attend the unpronounceable Verslunarmannahelgi (Labour Day) party in Iceland. Head out to the even remoter Westmann Islands, where, on the main island of Heimaey, the local population sets up camp in a valley and parties the night away on a tasty dinner of boiled puffin and serious alcohol.

Good Clean Scots Fun

Watch men in skirts throw very large logs about at Highland Games all over Scotland, with pipe bands, hammer flinging, tug o'war and bagpipes galore.

Redneck Hoedown

Witness the unforgettable Redneck Olympics in East Dublin, Georgia, at the beginning of July. With such charming events as the hubcap hurl, the mud-pit belly flop and bobbing for pigs' trotters, the brash trailer park vibe is irresistible and you'll soon be line dancing with the best of 'em.

kooky pursuits

The summer not only brings out the best festivals, but also some of the strangest. If you get a kick out of quirky, consider participating in these.

:: Swamp Soccer Championships (Finland) Sticky, swampy, mucky fun.[R]

:: La Tomatina Festival (Buñol, Spain) To honour St Louis, tens of thousands of people engage in a mass tomato fight, leaving rivers of tomato juice – up to a foot deep – running through town.

:: Cheese Rolling Contest (Cooper's Hill, Gloucestershire) Competitors race down the hill after a 7lb Double Gloucester cheese, which reaches up to 70mph.[R]

:: Sao Joao Festival (Porto, Portugal) In humorous homage to St John, patron saint of lovers, men and women hit those they find attractive over the head with plastic hammers.

:: Gilroy Garlic Festival (California) The world's largest garlic festival, attended by up to two million visitors and inaugurated with the lighting up of a 25-foot garlic bulb. Pass the mints, please.[R]

the bands played on

If you've tired of the same old line-up of tried and tested British rock festivals, venture out for alternative musical treats.[R]

:: **Roskilde Festival** (Denmark) This festival is immensely famous and famously immense. Big-name bands play over seven stages and several intoxicating days.[R]

:: **Fiberfib Rock Festival** (Valencia, Spain) The great location near the beach means you can spend the evenings floating in a sea of people and the scorching July days floating in the sea.[R]

:: **Wave-Gotik Treffen Festival** (Leipzig, Germany) Don your black eye shadow and roam amongst the 20,000 Goths who commune for the Wave-Gotik Treffen festival in May or June each year.[R]

:: **Fuji Rocks** (Japan) The incredible Fuji Rocks festival in July has Mount Fuji as its backdrop, helicopter rides over the festival site and thousands of Japanese bright young things.[R]

:: **Love Parade** (Berlin, Germany) Hit the road with the world's largest street party at the Love Parade, where millions revel to the sound of top-notch DJs.[R]

:: **Sziget Festival** (Budapest, Hungary) This festival runs for a whole week in August on an island in the middle of the Danube. Around 750 performers strut their stuff on 160 acres at this massive event where, in 2006, the world record for the largest ever cow mosaic was set. Those crazy Hungarians.[R]

:: **The Oxegen Festival** (County Kildare, Ireland) Crowds of over 80,000 per day show up in July for a stellar line-up and good old Irish craic.[R]

:: **Exit Festival** (Serbia) Demonstrating the Serbian reputation for wild partying, the Exit Festival is held in July at the picturesque Petrovaradin Fortress in Novi Sad.[R]

:: **Fez Festival of World Sacred Music** (Morocco) Held in June, the famous Fez Festival of World Sacred Music hosts spiritually slanted performances from across the world. [R]

:: **Savolinna Opera Festival** (Finland) For those who prefer Carmen to Coldplay, don't miss the Savolinna Opera Festival, where top names perform in June and July in an atmospheric castle setting.[R]

autumn

Indian Lights
Celebrate Divali, the dazzling Festival of Lights, in India along with millions of Hindus, Sikhs and Jains.

Reflect by Day, Feast by Night
Head to Cairo during Ramadan. During this period of fasting and reflection the city is quiet during the daytime, but comes alive at night with feasting in colourful open-air tents.

Whoop It Up In NYC
Take a break New York-style for the awesome Village Halloween Parade (31 October) or Macy's famous Thanksgiving Parade in November.[R]

Drunken Revelry En Masse
Drown your autumn blues at Oktoberfest in Munich, the world's largest beer festival. Begun in 1810 to celebrate a royal marriage, it was so popular (now with an annual consumption five million litres of beer in a fortnight) that it became an annual affair.[R]

Burn It
Live the communal life for a week at Burning Man in arid Nevada.[R]

DIY Partying
When summer's over and there are months to wait until the next bank holiday, what better choice for cheer than seizing a weekend and hosting your own autumn soiree?

food, glorious food

There are enough food festivals each year in Britain to fill your calendar, but the cream of the crop are almost all held during the autumn months when the year's harvest yields its richest pickings.

In early September, there's the **Ludlow Marches Food Festival**, with strong Shropshire ales and a seven-mile walking route along which you can sample a trail of culinary delights. Down south the **Devon Celebration of Food** runs throughout October with about 200 events across the counties to attract the galloping gourmet. Some of the most exciting include chocolate letterboxing – you get a chocolate reward if you complete the outdoor paper trail – and a tower-building contest using just spaghetti and marshmallows. Up north, there's the **Manchester Food and Drink Festival**, where you can attend a Chateau Biryani course to learn which wines best accompany Indian food. And almost wherever you are in the UK, you're sure to find autumnal festival stalls serving Slow Food (p104), organic oysters, or a mean Sloe Gin.[R]

winter
revel in film

Winter's the time for dimming the lights, grabbing the popcorn and donning your critic's hat at ten of the world's best cold-weather film festivals.

1. **International Documentary Festival** Amsterdam

2. **Black Nights Film Festival** Tallinn, Estonia

3. **London Children's Film Festival**

4. **Taipei Golden Horse Film Festival**

5. **Sundance Festival** Utah

6. **Slamdance Festival** Sundance Festival alternative, also in Utah

7. **Clermont-Ferrand Short Film Festival** France

8. **Bradford Animation Festival** Yorkshire

9. **Cinemagic Festival** Belfast

10. **Docudays Beirut International Documentary Festival**

a fiery new year

In Scotland and the North of England a few unique ancient traditions – all involving fire – are still enacted on New Year's Eve. Not something to attempt when you've taken early to the single malt.

:: **Hogmanay Stonehaven Fireball Festival** (Scotland) This traditional festival involves 60 marchers who perilously swing 16-pound fireballs on wires above their heads.

:: **Flambeaux Procession** (Comrie, Scotland) Tayside villagers march with blazing torches before throwing them onto the bonfire in the village square.

:: **Allendale Fire Ceremony** (Northumberland) Marchers carry flaming barrels of tar above their heads in a ritual dating back to pagan times.

:: **Burn the Old Year Out** (Biggar, Scotland) Biggar celebrates with a massive bonfire in the town square. During WWII they made do with lighting a candle in a tin can to make sure the tradition survived.[R]

go to the carnival

Celebrating the end of winter, perhaps with origins in the Roman festival of Saturnalia, there's Carnival fun aplenty across the globe.

:: **Carnival** (Rio de Janeiro, Brazil) Dance the night away at the carnival of carnivals for three raucous days at the end of February.

:: **Carnival** (Olinda, Spain) Share your pavement space with bonecos (huge papier-mâché figures) and preening travestis (transvestite paraders) in this normally sedate Spanish seaside town.

:: **Carnevale** (Venice, Italy) Revel in masked balls, sedate celebrations dating back to 1268, and gape at the period costumes in the crush of Piazza San Marco.[R]

:: **City Winter Carnival** (Quebec, Canada) For more frosty frolics visit the biggest winter carnival in the world; a flurry of dog sled rides, snow baths, ice sculpting and night-time parades.[R]

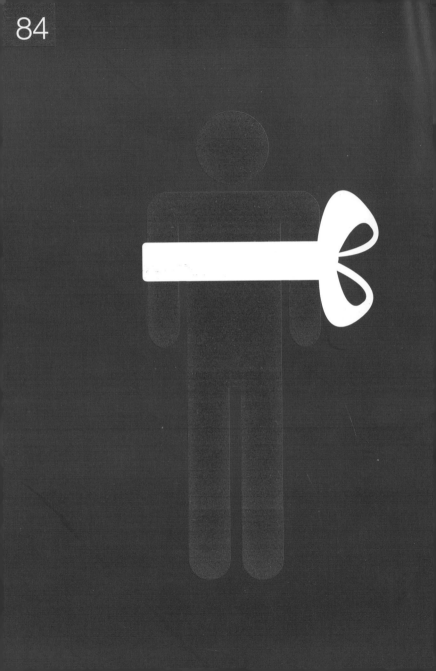

give

We make a living by what we do, but we make a life by what we give
– Winston Churchill

A growing number of people are choosing to spend some of their free time volunteering overseas, whether on an organized 'eco-holiday' or an independently arranged trip with one of hundreds of small private charities.

With 132 days to seize, surely you could give a few away to a worthy cause, whether on the opposite side of the globe or closer to home?

weekend

Dig It Up

Get down and dirty with a teaspoon at an archaeological dig. Current Archaeology offers a searchable database of voluntary and training digs across Britain. Discover the remains of a Roman villa, Bronze Age burial site or medieval manor – though you'll probably be asked to surrender any buried treasure you unearth.[R]

Friendly Furry Helpers

If you have a friendly cat or dog at home, you could both benefit the community by getting it registered with Pets as Therapy, a charity that sends volunteers along with their pets to visit nursing homes, hospitals and hospices. The charity coordinates almost half a million visits each year, bringing unconditional love and licks to isolated and lonely.[R]

Make a Difference

Become a Community Service Volunteer. CSV offers a wide range of community-based projects – including their London-based 'GO' project, which offers no-commitment volunteering at schools, city farms, hospitals and parks – as well as organising the annual 'Make a Difference Day', when over 100,000 people across the UK participate in all kinds of voluntary projects.[R]

online resources

According to Volunteering England 22 million adults in the UK are engaged in formal volunteering work each year, with 90 million hours of formal voluntary work performed each week. To join the growing ranks of Britain's volunteers search volunteer directories online. You might offer a foster home to an unwanted dog, become a circus assistant, or ride a tandem bicycle with a blind person.

:: **Volunteer Centre** Find the two-week – or two-year – opportunity that's right for you, with links to all the major voluntary organisations such as the Peace Corps, Trekforce and VSO (Voluntary Service Overseas).[R]

:: **Experience Corps** Match your skills and experience to over 400,000 voluntary opportunities with work ranging from helping to protect endangered Exmoor ponies, to driving duties for the British Red Cross, to befriending AIDS patients at an East London hospital.[R]

:: **Timebank** This charity connects British people with volunteering opportunities in their local community and has so far attracted 220,000 people into the world of voluntary work. You could become a mentor for stressed-out parents or refugees, or befriend isolated elderly people. Register with Timebank and they'll come up with an opportunity to suit your interests and available spare time in your local area.[R]

:: **Do It** You can search by area of interest, geographical area and the exact time you have free to volunteer.[R]

> A man's true wealth hereafter is the good that he does in this world to his fellows – Moliere

Give a Green Weekend
Spend a weekend or two at the Eden Project in Cornwall, which aims to educate people about major environmental issues. It contains more than one million plants, as well as thought-provoking art works and installations. Eden welcomes volunteers, but needs them to commit to at least 72 hours per year because of the training and support involved.[R]

Keep Cyclists Safe
Become a Volunteer Ranger or take part in a weekend work camp for Sustrans, the UK's leading Sustainable Transport Charity. Responsible for the National Cycle Network, which encompasses over 10,000 miles of safe cycling routes across Britain, Sustrans's volunteer rangers inspect routes near their homes, ensuring they stay safe and attractive for cyclists. If you want to work up a sweat, work camps offer you the opportunity to help Sustrans clock up a few more miles by building cycling trails.[R]

Hug a Tree
Volunteer with the Forestry Commission, which has a whole host of vacancies across the UK. Build mountain bike trails, help with conservation work, litter pick amongst trees, become a volunteer ranger, information officer or an expert on Ospreys.[R]

Free Festivals
Work as a steward, administrator or ticket-tearer at a weekend music, food, literary, film or arts festival. See 'Party' (p71) for a few festival ideas, or find a festival that appeals to you and enquire directly about their non-paid opportunities.

Help Heritage
Spend a weekend away with the National Trust, volunteering on one of its two-day working holidays, or look into regular weekend opportunities at its stately homes, parks and gardens across the country.[R]

Teach English Around the World
Take a weekend TEFL (Teaching English as a Foreign Language) course, after which you can competently and confidently volunteer almost anywhere in the world as an English teacher.[R]

week

Get Wet, Do Good

Get physical with a Volunteer Outdoor Week at the REO Whitewater Rafting Resort outside Vancouver in Canada. In exchange for room, board and adventure activity experience, you'll contribute 50 hours of camp maintenance on the beautiful British Columbian Nahatlatch River.[R]

Help Save the World

Take a week in the great outdoors with the venerable British Trust for Conservation Volunteers (BTCV) which organises week-long working holidays at home and further afield. Lay hedges in Cheshire, help out with wetland protection in Bavaria, work on footpaths in Lesotho, or plant trees in Cameroon.[R]

¿Habla Ingles?

If you're a compulsive talker, put your skill – or curse – to good use with a week's break in a picturesque Spanish village in return for pure, unadulterated conversation. At Pueblo Ingles you can become an 'Anglo', a sort of casual English teacher, whose only job is to chat the hind legs off a group of Spaniards keen to be immersed in real, non-classroom English.[R]

Assist Exotic Communities

Check out the projects on offer with Global Vision International, which has opportunities for week-long volunteer placements in exotic locations, including short-term community projects in Guatemala and Honduras, where you'll help build energy-efficient stoves or plant crops in indigenous communities, with Spanish lessons thrown in for good measure.[R]

WWOOF Away!

Sow seeds in Slovenia, pick berries in Bulgaria or experience permaculture in Portugal when you volunteer on an organic farm with WWOOF (World Wide Opportunities on Organic Farms).[R]

A Hand for Four-Legged Friends

Help out at an animal shelter. There are dozens of places in need of helping hands, so pick your favourite creature and you're sure to find a sanctuary glad to receive assistance. You could care for cats and dogs in Cairo, with the Society for the Protection of Animal Rights in Egypt, or hang out with horses, pot bellied pigs and emus at the Mossburn Centre in Scotland.[R]

fortnight **or more**

Unforgettable Help
Get intimate with those most majestic of creatures with several weeks volunteering at an elephant sanctuary. There's Kegalle in Sri Lanka, Mwaluganje in Kenya, or Riddle's Elephant Sanctuary in Arkansas, which offers month-long internships and courses in elephant management for pachydermophiles.[R]

Don't Desert the Desert
Head south for a two-week stint at Sunseed Desert Technology in arid southern Spain, which relies on volunteers to keep up their dry-land management work. You'll learn all about sustainable living, and can try your hand at dry stone walling or operating a solar cooker.[R]

Twitcher's Paradise
Revel in the tranquillity of birdsong on the Royal Society for the Protection of Birds residential voluntary warden scheme, during which you might be surveying, greeting visitors, or taking part in conservation work at one of its 39 reserves nationwide.[R]

Helping Out in Africa
Take a look at the volunteer opportunities offered by Ikando, founded by a couple of keen volunteers who found volunteering both difficult to arrange and costly to undertake. Most volunteer placements require a minimum of a four-week commitment, though some, like drama teaching at the Children's Christian Storehouse in Accra, or assisting in a Ghanaian School for the Deaf classroom, have fortnight-long posts on offer.[R]

Lending a Hand in the Himalaya
If you're inspired by the colour of Kathmandu, there's a wide range of volunteering options available in Nepal. There's Volunteer Society Nepal offering multi-week placements teaching English, helping out at an orphanage, or, if you have medical training, working at a local hospital. Info Nepal offers similar placements, but shorter and two-week stints can be arranged, whilst Hands for Help Nepal also offers a variety of programmes, including a two-week summer work camp and a fortnight's health, education and environmental programme.[R]

Empower Village Women
Work on women's development programmes or on HIV/AIDS education projects at the Sachabu Care Foundation in rural Ghana, which manages grassroots women's empowerment projects and educates villagers on sexual health.[R]

ongoing opportunities

Get Acquainted with an Ass

Become a regular at one of the UK's many donkey sanctuaries. The Elizabeth Svendsen Trust for Children and Donkeys has five centres across Britain and welcomes volunteers to feed, lead and groom – though you'll have to take a day-long introductory Donkey Care Course first.[R]

Become a Good Samaritan

The Samaritans rely entirely on volunteers to staff its phone lines. You'll need to be a good listener, and have about three to four hours per week to spare and be able to do one overnight shift per month. You'll receive comprehensive training before you take to the phone lines. Alternatively, volunteer for Samaritans' festival branch, which provides tents at festivals for the same confidential emotional support.[R]

Clown Around

The whole world loves a clown and hospital clowns are no exception. A legion of volunteer Clown Doctors roam wards, dispensing smiles, laughs and magic tricks to both children and adult patients. If you have a dramatic background, a sympathetic demeanour and a couple of free afternoons per week, the Theodora Children's Trust and Clown Doctors can provide information on how to start dispensing the magical medicine of laughter.[R]

think big:
behold the turtle

7 days

There's a staggeringly slim one-in-one-thousand chance of a baby turtle making it all the way to adulthood, so well intentioned volunteers are needed across the globe to ensure their safe passage to the sea. Be a week-long 'green turtle guardian' at the Banyan Tree resort on Vabbinfaru in the Maldives (you can also adopt a turtle for £42 per year) and, if a nest hatches, you'll be woken in the middle of the night to escort the tiny creatures safely down to the water's edge.[R]

30 days

Help endangered sea turtles in Kenya by a stint at one of its several turtle charities. Watamu Turtle Watch welcomes volunteers willing to immerse themselves in its various tagging, conservation and education projects, as well as to participate in the rehabilitation of sick turtles, surveying and replanting programmes. With year-round sunshine, and the opportunity to experience Kenya's stunning underwater environment, it's an educational, emotional experience, with the added opportunity to acquire a fantastic tan.[R]

132 days

Head to Costa Rica's stunning Pacific coast to work intensively with Baula turtles, the largest turtle species in the world, and Olive Ridley turtles, both of which are severely threatened due to beach development, egg harvesting, fishing, pollution and the demand for turtle leather and meat. The work, much of which is rotational night shifts, includes preparing and repairing nests, patrolling beaches, recording numbers of turtles and eggs, and taking nests' temperatures, while simple accommodation is in temporary shelters erected only for the turtle season.

ecotourism & sustainable travel

Many working holidays label themselves eco-friendly, but what does ecotourism really involve? According to the International Ecotourism Society, ecotourism is "responsible travel to natural areas that conserves the environment and improves the well-being of local people". When you consider signing up for a project, it's worth considering whether it fits the bill according to IES standards. The ideal project should:

:: minimise impact

:: build environmental and cultural awareness and respect

:: provide positive experiences for both guests and hosts

:: provide direct financial benefits for conservation

:: provide financial benefits and empowerment for local people

:: raise sensitivity to social, cultural, political and environmental climate

:: support international human rights and labour agreements

Visit the IES website for more background on the principles of ecotourism and links to a host of eco-projects.[R]

the perils of voluntourism

The phenomenon of responsible, or meaningful, travel means that even people who in the past would have spent a fortnight sunning themselves in the Canaries are now exchanging their sun cream for a shovel, or Caipirinha for a classroom.

But is voluntourism always beneficial to the local community? Some people argue that many of the holiday companies selling 'responsible' working holidays are simply out to make a buck from public sympathy or guilt, and that a two-week volunteering stint somewhere isn't really much use, as it gives neither the volunteer nor the community they find themselves in time to adjust. Equally, some destinations aren't keen on the voluntourist turning up on their doorstep; several years ago, litter-picking trips on the Nile were cancelled after the Egyptian Tourist Board complained that Egypt was being portrayed as a third-world country.

Certainly, some organisations are better at providing support for volunteers than others, and some projects are better conceived and provide more meaningful results. So before you book with a tour operator, it's worth asking these questions:

:: Are there any reports available on the success of previous projects?

:: Is the project run in conjunction with locals themselves?

Bearing these things in mind will help you find a place, and a project, in which you can really help out.[R]

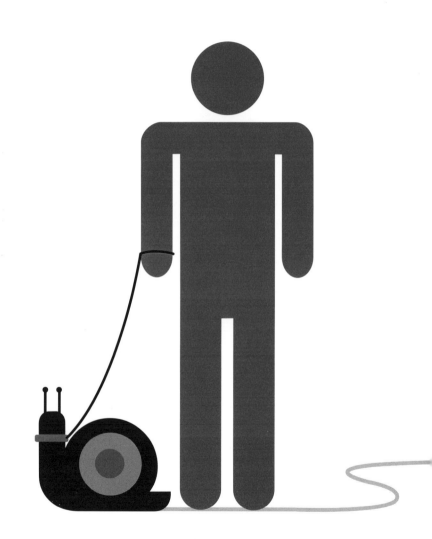

slow
down

The slower you go, the farther you will be
– Russian proverb

Stop rushing from place to place, errand to errand, work to home and back again. Walk to work if you usually cycle; cycle to work if you usually take your motorbike; go by bus or train if you usually drive. You'll find things you have never noticed before – a great new restaurant, a hidden junk shop, a tiny, forgotten statue commemorating a long-ago event. And you may even find yourself some time to think.

bank holiday

Slow Motion
Find a walking or biking trail near you and head out for a leisurely day in the open air. Take a thermos of coffee, a picnic lunch and a good book to enjoy over a long, languid lunch, or – in chillier months – plan ahead by choosing a route with a good pub to stop off at along the way.[R]

Real Food
Enjoy the tactile experience of handling, sniffing and tasting fresh produce. Forsake the supermarket and buy all your groceries the old-fashioned way: cheese from the cheese shop, vegetables from the greengrocer, bread from that bakery you've been meaning to drop into, and flowers and herbs from a fragrant market stall.

Go Batty
At dusk all over Britain dozens of these furry, flying creatures swoop out of their daytime haunts for a night of flitting about beneath the moon. Many nature reserves offer guided bat walks; try spooky Newark Park Bat Walk in Gloucestershire, the Bat Walk at Renishaw Hall in Derbyshire, or a Bat Watch at Glenbranter Forest in Argyll Forest Park, Scotland.[R]

> A good traveller has no fixed plans, and is not intent on arriving – Lao Tzu

Gather Nature's Bounty

Do lunch the slow way by treating yourself to a gourmet forage in the forest. Award-winning chef Matt Tebutt will take you deep into the Welsh countryside to hunt for samphire, hazelnuts, wimberries and elderberries, and then back to his restaurant to sample the fruits of your labours.[R]

Explore Your Home Town

Skip that day trip to Venice and take a walking tour of a town or city near you instead. Even if you think you know your local area well, you'll discover hidden treasures, forgotten nooks and crannies, and start to see your home turf in a completely different light.

Spot a Sea Mammal

Go whale or dolphin watching off the coasts of Southern England, Wales or Scotland. There's no guarantee you'll spot any of these majestic watery mammals, but it's fun to hang out on the deck, breathing in the sea air and scanning the horizon for fins, tails and blow-holes.[R]

dine in the dark

Eating becomes a much slower affair when you can't see a thing...

The concept of dining in the dark, which maintains that you better savour the subtle flavours of food when you can't see it and when you're forced to eat more slowly, is popular across Europe and North America, and there's a London restaurant completely devoted to it. Dans Le Noir in Clerkenwell has a dark bar, restaurant and blind waiters to act as your guides; once inside the pitch-black dining area, you have to stay put – for fear of head-on collisions – and you summon your waiter by calling out their name. So far, so good – but it might be one to avoid on a first date, and we suggest you don't wear your best white shirt.[R]

> We wander for distraction, but we travel for fulfilment – Hilaire Belloc

weekend

As Slow as Melting Chocolate

Take a cookery course in chocolate making or patisserie, two very complex arts that really illustrate how patience and practice make perfect. The Ashburton Cookery School in Dartmoor offers one-day classes in patisserie and puddings, leaving you a second day to enjoy the glorious national park. Or for something more decadent, head to world renowned chocolatier Lenôtre, in Paris, where patisserie classes and an 'A-Z of chocolate' course are available. It's definitely a case of taking your time though: it takes over four hours to make a Lenôtre 'all chocolate' cake.[R]

Make a Mini-Epic

Buy a Super 8 camera, projector and film splicer, and make a film the old-fashioned way. Since every film cartridge is only a few minutes long, silent and has to be sent off to the lab for developing, the process is lengthy and the results uncertain – making it much more fun than simply switching on your palmcorder.

More Than a Treasure Hunt

Try a weekend 'letterboxing' in Cumbria, Scotland or Dartmoor – a great way to spend a slow weekend outdoors. A mixture of orienteering and treasure hunting, which involves searching for 'letterboxes' containing rubber stamps, it's a low-tech version of the popular geocaching. Started in 1854 in Dartmoor, the modern version of letterboxing involves following clues to find hidden boxes, which contain a visitor's book to sign and a rubber stamp for marking your own personal letterboxing 'passport'. In the Lake District, there are letterboxes somewhere in Grizedale Forest, Skiddaw Forest and on Helvellyn, Skaffel Pike and Hallin Fell, whilst on Dartmoor there are thousands to locate.[R]

Barge Into Tranquillity

Watch the world go by from the water, with a lazy weekend narrowboating along Britain's countryside or city canals.[R]

Bite by Leisurely Bite

Get into the Slow Food movement, started in 1986 by Italian food journalist Carlo Petrini. It shuns fast food and promotes local cuisines, organic production, and the enjoyment of the slow art of cooking. Now with over 80,000 members worldwide, the movement is taking the culinary world by storm.[R]

24/7

Although our lives now revolve around the separation of our days into week and weekend, the seven-day week has actually only been around for about 1600 years.

Unlike days, which come and go with night-time, and months, which rise and fall with the cycle of the moon, weeks and weekends have no clear manifestation in the physical world – unless you count traffic jams on Friday night and dragging heels on Monday morning. The ancient Greeks and Egyptians, for example, split their months into three cycles of ten days; the ancient Mayans, into phases of thirteen.

So was our seven-day week the arbitrary invention of evil industrialists who wanted to make sure we spent the majority of our lives working? Not necessarily. Modern chronobiologists have discovered that the human body demonstrates a 'circaseptan rhythm', or seven-day beat, which involves tiny variations in heart rate, blood pressure and response to infections. Moreover, a week-long cycle did exist in the Middle East long before the coming of the Romans…and just take a quick glance at the book of Genesis to remember that even God had a rest at the weekend.

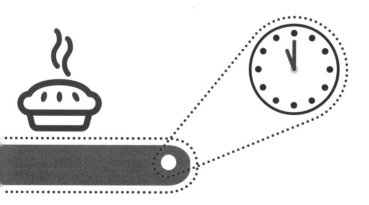

week

Make Like a Local, Abroad

Instead of the usual weekend city break, rent an apartment and stay for a week. Immerse yourself in a routine – buying breakfast, making lunch, adapting your home routine to another city. Visit museums at a leisurely pace, browse shops and wander the streets of lesser-known parts of town. Take a couple of books set in the city to get under its skin, and go to your local bar every night for a week; by the end of it, you'll be conversing with locals and feel like part of the scene. Try Istanbul, Cairo, Rome or New York City for starters

Relaxation, Pure and Natural

Soak up the rays on eco-friendly Chumbe Island, sandwiched between Zanzibar and the coast of Tanzania, where all the buildings are made of natural materials and there's not a minibar or TV in sight to distract you from taking your time to wind down completely. Snorkel above a pristine reef or simply snooze in a hammock, as the days glide leisurely by.[R]

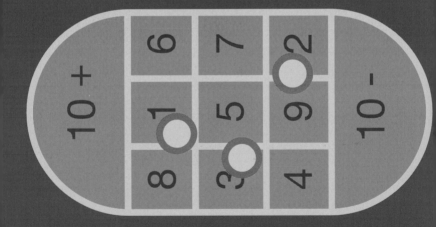

why **fly when you could…**

…hit the rails

Train travel is rarely the fastest way to get about, but for a touch of the romantic and evocative nothing beats watching the world go by from a gently swaying train berth.

You could spend a merry week exploring the four corners of the British Isles, alighting at modern and Victorian stations, and seeing cities from their back gardens. Or you could take a rail pass somewhere you might otherwise travel by car, like Australia or Japan. You could also choose the challenge of the unknown and unplanned; head to the country of your choice and take the next available train to wherever it happens to be heading. Hop off at the end of the line or wherever takes your fancy en route.

For the sybarite there's the lure of one of the world's most memorable train lines, on which you can live a life of regal splendour. Live like a Maharaja on board the **Palace on Wheels** across dazzling Rajasthan, or satisfy those Agatha Christie aspirations by hopping the Venice-bound **Orient Express**. Take the **Trans-Manchurian Express** from Moscow to Beijing, or go for broke on a five-star luxury trip on the poshest train ride in the world, **Rovos Rail**, from Cape Town to Dar-es-Salaam.[R]

…take to the high seas

Speaking of romance, try a ship voyage on a freight or container ship. A journey across the Atlantic will take about 10 days, depending on the type of ship. Southampton to Hong Kong will take a little over three weeks, whilst Rotterdam to Los Angeles will mean just over five weeks traversing the waves. The Cruise People offer a comprehensive booking service for this alternative type of cruise – no cheesy dinner dances, cabaret shows or petanque on-deck.[R]

fortnight **or more**

Challenge for Charity

Drive the charity Plymouth–Banjul challenge in a car worth less than £100. A low-budget alternative to the famous Paris–Dakar rally which takes drivers about 21 days. Surviving cars are auctioned off in aid of local Gambian charities.[R]

Walk It

Take a week's leisurely walk along the Great Ocean Walk in southeastern Australia between Apollo Bay and Glenample Homestead, near the Twelve Apostles. This 91km trail offers seven hike-in campsites and takes in not only the tallest cliffs in mainland Australia, but shimmering waterfalls, forests of ferns and the odd koala. Stop in at the Cape Otway Centre for Conservation Ecology, where injured marsupials are rehabilitated, marvel at flocks of king parrots, laze on deserted beaches and take afternoon tea at the oldest lighthouse in Australia.[R]

Clip-Clop

Spend a fortnight clip-clopping down the open roads of Ireland in a horse-drawn carriage enjoying spectacular scenery at a restful walking pace, and overnighting at equi-friendly pubs, farms and guesthouses along the way.[R]

the journey is the destination

I travel not to go anywhere, but to go. I travel for travel's sake.
– Robert Louis Stevenson

As long as there has been life, there have been travellers. From monarch butterflies migrating between the Rocky Mountains and Mexico, to Emperor penguins marching hundreds of miles to ancestral breeding grounds, the most diverse species see travel as a necessity – and humans are no exception. There were ancient nomadic tribes, medieval pilgrims, 17th-century naval explorers and Victorian gents on the Grand Tour. A 19th-century doctor would regularly prescribe travel as a cure for melancholy; gypsy and circus communities are based on being on the move; and since the 1960s modern backpackers have continued the ancient travelling tradition, making their way through Africa, Asia and the Americas.

In recent years, we've seen the re-emergence of perpetual travellers. There are those who sell up, buy a boat and take to the seas, and the two million or so senior citizens in the USA who've bought a motor home and are spending their twilight years chasing the sun. As Anatole France once said: "Wandering re-establishes the original harmony which once existed between man and the universe."

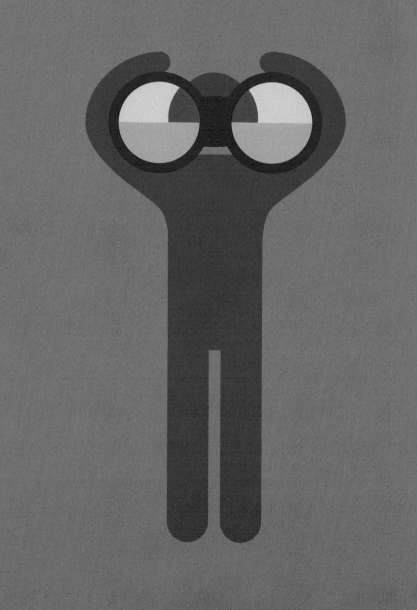

new
horizons

Learn as if you were going to live forever
— Mahatma Gandhi

Seizing your 132 days isn't just about exciting one-off activities. You can also use some of that time to experiment with a new hobby or discover new skills. There are literally tonnes of options out there, ranging from the fairly standard to the entirely unconventional. Who knows? You might find that secret tango dancer, falconer or nudist that's been hiding deep down inside.

evening

Make 'em Laugh

Take a comedy improvisation class to release the Morecambe, Wise or Izzard from within. Evening and weekend workshops take place all over the UK to unleash your lightning wit and thrilling repartee, and give you the ability to put the cast of Whose Line is it Anyway to shame.[R]

At the Gee-Gees

Get your pulse pumping with a trip to the races. There's nothing like a little flutter on the ponies to get you oohing, grimacing and yelling "Go on, my son!" along with the geezers.[R]

Star of the Circus

Try dangling from the end of a very high swing by taking trapeze or corde lisse (acrobatics on an aerial rope) lessons, which will improve your stamina, strength and self-confidence – and make a change from an hour on the treadmill.

Throw a Pot

Take yourself – and your kids, if you have any – for an evening of mucky fun at a pottery workshop. Throwing, thumping and digging your nails into a large lump of clay is a satisfyingly therapeutic activity, and you can proudly take home your (wonky) teapot afterwards.

> Winston Churchill's pastimes included painting, laying bricks and farming.

Two to Tango

Grab a partner and enrol in tango lessons, probably the sultriest, suavest, sexiest dance ever danced. Once you've donned your stilettos or borsalino and learnt to twist dramatically across the dancefloor, you can head to a salon, where you'll find dancers of all ages and nationalities sweeping theatrically about. And if tango's not your style, try Bhangra, bellydancing, ballroom or bossa nova instead.

Strum, Blow or Beat Something

Learn a musical instrument. If piano, violin or guitar just don't do it for you, try an unusual alternative. For example, you could do like the kilted and learn the bagpipes, try out the clavichord, one of the very oldest keyboard instruments, or dabble in Arabic instruments such as the oud, daf and ney.[R]

Slave It Out

If you're sick of your usual yoga DVD, try something a little different with Slavercise, a fitness fad currently sweeping New York, and available for Brits on DVD, run by Miss Victoria, a famous NYC dominatrix. Prepare to be put through your physical and mental paces in a combination of humiliation and hard work – all for a good healthy cause.[R]

one perfect (outside) hour

"Whilst sitting at my desk during yet another working lunch, it suddenly struck me that I'd hardly moved from my computer all morning and I had a sudden burst of inspiration: an Outside Hour, simply to get lots of people outside in the fresh air one lunchtime. They could picnic, play frisbee in the park, go rowing on the river; it didn't matter, so long as they went outdoors. I got in touch with local radio and even the mayor and the idea really took off; people even arranged guided walks and free pizza for those who made it outside. On the day itself, hundreds of people did leave their chairs for an hour, despite bad weather. And even though it was only one single lunch hour, I think it made people realise how easy it is to forget the world outside the office window."

– Ellen Pearce, Manager, Cambridge

weekend

Buzz Off
Become an apiarist. Get acquainted with drones, queens and smokers by learning the art of beekeeping – and always have your own personal supply of honey for your toast and tea.[R]

Tame the Wild Outdoors
Take a weekend 'essentials' survival course, where you'll learn animal tracking, navigation, firelighting using fungi (seriously) and a gamut of other skills to keep you safe if you happen to be lost in the great British wilderness. Courses are held by the UK Survival School in the heart of the scenic Brecon Beacons.[R]

For the Birds
Try your hand at that most noble of ancient pursuits, falconry, learning your way around leather gauntlets, peregrine falcons and jesses. There are dozens of centres across the UK where you can try an afternoon, day-long or weekend taster to see if the hawking spirit catches you, after which you can command owls, vultures and eagles like knights of yore.[R]

Get Your Hands Dirty

Think of allotments and you probably envisage old men with cloth caps, dirty fingernails and a piece of string holding up their trousers. But nowadays, weeding and seeding at an allotment is a calming way to experience the pleasure of growing your own organic fruit, herbs and vegetables, along with the peace of being away from it all. Have a look at Allotment Growing or Allotments UK to find out how to find, manage and make your allotment flourish.[R]

Go Underground

If you're one of those people who relishes the thrill of exploring dark, spooky spaces, spend a weekend exploring Britain's subterranean world: there are abandoned mines, caves, bunkers and other assorted dingy holes all over the place, and a large number of UK enthusiasts keen on getting into them. Go to Dark Places, to find out the hows, whys and wheres of this slightly sinister hobby.[R]

Do Your Own Adaptation

Fancy yourself as the next Charlie Kaufman? Then take an intensive course in screenwriting with charismatic, cranky Robert McKee. A three-day intensive seminar, usually held over a weekend, involves long days of frantic note-taking, intent listening and being shouted at if you arrive late. McKee's students have included 26 Academy Award winners and a whole host of Hollywood notables.[R]

week

Tree-Top Hideaways

You don't have to be a 10-year-old to build a tree house. Get some tree climbing experience in Cornwall or take a week's inspiration from the Green Magic Nature Resort in Kerala, southern India, and then learn how to build your own with The Treehouse Guide. You're then fully equipped to create your ultimate retreat within the boughs of a tree, fitted out with your favourite forbidden fruits: a well-stocked minibar, an oversized bed and a stash of luxury snacks.[R]

Quirky Getaways

Find out more about the UK's most unusual buildings – by staying in them. Try a break at one of the Landmark Trust's properties: there's a 200-year-old pineapple shaped folly in Scotland, a former Cornish arsenic mine, a Norfolk water tower, a Staffordshire railway station, and a radio hut on the island of Lundy.[R]

Get Your Gear Off

Get back to basics by discovering naturism. The British Naturism society has a staggering 16,000 members, all of whom enjoy whipping their kit off in the great outdoors. You can take a naturist caravanning holiday, join one of its 130 Sun Clubs, or let it all hang out underwater at a naturist swim club.[R]

Befriend the Big Five

Head to South Africa to learn how to elephant wrangle or hand-rear a rhino at the Game Capture School in Faerie Glen, Pretoria. Courses are for professionals and amateurs alike, after which you can choose to stay on as a volunteer at the Wildlife Hospital where you'll be feeding and mucking out injured animals, patrolling the farm's perimeters in search of poachers and learning rehabilitation techniques.[R]

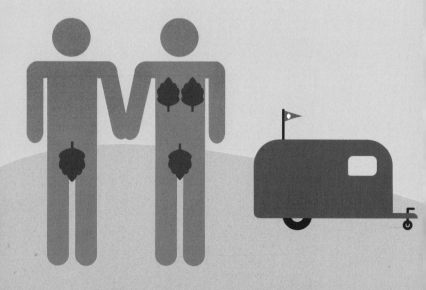

invest in seizing your days

Commit to making the most of your time off by investing in property abroad. In the short term you'll learn (or have to teach yourself) loads of new skills ranging from how to lay floorboards to negotiating your way around dealing with local builders. In the long term having property abroad will be a tidy incentive for you to get away from the humdrum and may even turn a profit for you in the future.

Although the days of buying up an old farmhouse in Provence or Tuscany for peanuts have long passed, there are still a number of alluring destinations quite close to home where you can buy yourself a crumbling wreck and then take time out to renovate it. Currently, the most popular places for investing in property are in eastern European locations which are now easily accessible by air from Britain.

Here's a quick guide to locating and buying the property of your dreams.

1. Grab a guidebook to the country you're considering and highlight the regions you're most interested in. Do you want isolation high up in the mountains, or somewhere close to the beach? A pied-à-terre in a bustling city or tranquillity in a rustic country village? Are you willing to take on a wreck and build from scratch, or are you more comfortable with renovations of the lick-of-paint variety?

2. Research the costs involved and the legalities of purchasing property abroad, and make careful note of any possible tax implications.

3. Trawl the websites of the major estate agents. Make a list of all the properties you're immediately drawn to and email each company for details of the exact location, extra photos and further information.

4. Organise a viewing visit – a cottage that looks perfect in the picture might be right next to a petrol station; on the other hand, a pile of crumbling stones might have the most picture-perfect location and potential. Many estate agents will also be able to advise you on the basic costs for reconstruction or refurbishment and recommend local building companies, as well as talk you through the procedure for acquiring a property.

In the 18th century, taxidermy was used to preserve specimens brought back from voyages to distant shores – Captain Cook's crew taxidermised creatures brought back from the New World. The technique was also extended to the preservation of pets – the Duchess of Richmond's African Grey parrot, dating back to 1702, still perches in Westminster Abbey. In the 19th century, taxidermy became popular as a way for keen hunters to show off their conquests.

With the help of artists Damien Hirst, Polly Morgan and Emily Mayer, taxidermy is trendy, back with a vengeance and attracting new recruits.

Alfred

dark tourism

Dark Tourism is the phrase that's been coined to describe the rising wave of tourists interested in visiting sites of tragedy, disaster, or sorrow: Ground Zero, Auschwitz-Birkenau, dead celebrities' crash sites, or tsunami-hit beaches. However, it's anything but a modern invention; in fact, Dark Tourists have been seeing the sights for centuries. Historically, pilgrimage sites were often places in which a saint or prophet had been painfully martyred, and during the 1815 Battle of Trafalgar the wealthy and curious were actually able to observe the battle itself from a safe distance. Today, Chernobyl is growing in popularity as a tourism site, where daytrips to the devastated reactor can be taken for around £120. But what is it that makes us want to observe the relics of what we'd never want to live through? For most, it's a mixture of reverence for the past, the thrill of voyeurism, and a contemplation of mortality. More than that, Dark Tourism sites have the power to teach us a poignant lesson in humanity's biggest mistakes and worst excesses.

fortnight or more

Appreciate the Outsiders

You don't have to be a Da Vinci to be an artist and amateur 'outsider' folk art is even becoming popular with the world's elite art collectors. Perhaps the most famous outsider art project is Nek Chand's Rock Garden of Chandigarh in India, 25 acres of jaw-dropping primitive sculptures and structures.[R]

Learn to Sign

Although Spanish or Chinese might be useful on your next big trip, you can use sign language at home too. British Sign offers a seven-week interactive online course to get yourself fully equipped to chat away with your hands.[R]

Go Eco

Take a series of residential courses at the Centre for Alternative Technology, Europe's leading eco-centre, to learn the basics of wind and solar power, straw bale house building and eco-design, and then apply those skills to your own home. The centre also accepts short- and long-term volunteers if you're really keen to be green.[R]

up in lights

7 days

If you're considering a career change, even a week can provide a good opportunity to get beneath the skin of your dream profession. For example, if the glamour of the movie industry beckons, offer your services as a runner for a film, commercial or TV production. While the reality is about as unglamorous as it gets – you'll probably spend a lot of time making tea, holding important people's coats and driving pieces of equipment about – it's a great chance to see whether this frenetically paced life is the one for you.

30 days

The next rung up the star-studded ladder to securing a new career in the entertainment industry is by getting some work experience or landing an internship. No longer just intended for students, work experience is nowadays a good form of on-the-job training for all; the BBC, for example, offers a wide range of unpaid opportunities lasting up to one month across its film and television departments. An internship will provide you with an invaluable insight into the workings of the industry, the chance to make crucial contacts and perhaps even a longer-term paid contract at the end.[R]

132 days

Take an intensive filmmaking course, learning everything from camera angles and budgeting to lighting techniques and dialogue writing, and come away with a clutch of short films for your new portfolio. A number of film schools offer practical courses, including the international New York Film Academy, the Asian Academy of Film and Television in India's Uttar Pradesh, and the UK's Brighton Film School. Britfilms has extensive listings of ongoing part-time and online courses across Britain, as well as longer-term full-time courses leading to Bachelor and Masters degrees and beyond.[R]

resources

Where possible, we've included resources to enable you to seize your days using the suggestions in this book. In some cases there is no resource that we would particularly recommend, so we'd encourage you to use your initiative (and your favourite search engine) to follow up on the inspiration provided in these pages.

For country-specific information, visit www.lonelyplanet.com/worldguide.

pages 6-7
Why Not Try?
www.london-marathon.co.uk
en.wikipedia.org/wiki/Vassa
www.peacecorpswriters.org

pages 8-9
To find out more about your rights at work, visit www.worksmart.org.uk/rights or www.oasis.gov.ie/employment

pages 26-27
There's Gold in Them Thar Streams
www.baile-an-or.ukfossils.co.uk/Baile-Fossils-Geology/how-to-pan.htm
www.leadminingmuseum.co.uk/Gold_Panning.htm
Wander a Windswept Beach
www.goodbeachguide.co.uk
www.adoptabeach.org.uk

pages 28-29
Get Lost
www.gwydir.demon.co.uk/jo/maze
Rummage for Rocks
www.jurassiccoast.com

pages 30-31
Start Small: Top 10 Mini Escapes
www.ukgraves.info
www.significantcemeteries.net
www.how-to-meditate.org
www.museums.co.uk
www.gagb.org.uk
www.lidos.org.uk
www.mypole.co.uk
www.londonschoolofstriptease.co.uk

pages 36-37
Sleeps with a Twist
www.ho-shi.co.jp
www.airstreameurope.com

pages 38-39
Spoil Yourself, Caribbean-Style
www.caribbeanclubs.net/thebeachhouse/index.html

pages 46-47
Hills, Dales, Glades & Brooks
www.woodland-trust.org.uk
It's a Riot
www.laughteryoga.org
Hug Some Sacred Stones
www.stonepages.com
Take the Plunge
www.outdoorswimmingsociety.com
Relaxation, Chinese-Style
www.taichifinder.co.uk

pages 48-49
Open Your Mind
www.taracentre.org.uk
Blessed Be the Silent
www.caldey-island.co.uk
Creative Study
www.photoactive.co.uk
Limber Body; Mind to Follow
www.yogaatwork.co.uk
The Art of Shutting Up
www.retreats.org.uk

pages 52-53
Purge Your Psyche
www.hoffmaninstitute.co.uk
Work for Your (Luxury) Supper
www.whitemountainretreat.com
Rewire Your Mind
www.hotcourses.com
www.nightcourses.com

pages 54-55
Thai-Style Reflection
www.chiva-som.com
www.thesanctuary-kpg.com
Sacred Pursuits
www.sacredtrust.org

pages 58-59
Go Ape
www.goape.co.uk
Try River Bugging
www.rafting.co.uk
A Risk-Free Plunge
www.airkix.com
www.bodyflight.com
Get Piste
www.ski.visitscotland.com
www.ifyouski.com/dryslopes
Extreme Cycling
www.forestry.gov.uk
Climb the Walls
www.thebmc.co.uk
www.ukclimbing.com
www.indoorclimbing.com/ireland.html
Have a Ball
www.zorbsouth.co.uk
www.chooseyourevent.com/profile.asp?cid=1023

pages 60-61
Go Fly a Kite
www.kitesurfing.org
Hit the Waves
www.rya.co.uk
Alpacas in Action
www.llamas.co.uk/Pages/llamatreks.htm

pages 62-63
Active Family Fun
www.outwardbound-uk.org

pages 64-65
Turkish Ascent
www.lycianway.com
Chilling with the Fish
www.apnea-academy.com
www.umbertopelizzari.com
Volcanoes & Vampires
www.riding-holidays.ro
Snow Breaks with a Difference
www.skileb.com

pages 66-67
Survivor!
www.bushmasters.co.uk
Outback Adventures
www.gibbriverbus.com.au

pages 68-69
20,000 Leagues Under the Sea
www.wildwings.co.uk
Camp it Up
www.tipis-indiens.com
www.angelisland.org
www.trellyn.co.uk
www.cottars.com

pages 74-75
One for Folk Folk
www.cheltenhamfestivals.com/jobs
Celebrate with the Celebs
www.festival-cannes.fr
Fire Up
www.edinburghguide.com/feats/beltane.htm
24hr Party People
www.wmcon.com

pages 76-77
The Bands Played On
www.roskilde-festival.dk
www.fiberfib.com
www.wave-gotik-treffen.de
www.fujirockfestival.com
www.sziget.hu
www.oxegen.ie
www.exitfest.org
www.loveparade.net
www.fesfestival.com
www.operafestival.fi

pages 78-79
Hippy Revelry
www.big-green-gathering.com
Kooky Pursuits
www.suopotkupallo.fi
www.cheese-rolling.co.uk
www.gilroygarlicfestival.com

pages 80-81
Whoop It Up In NYC
www.halloween-nyc.com
Drunken Revelry En Masse
http://www.oktoberfest.de/en

Burn It
www.burningman.com
Food, Glorious Food
www.foodfestival.co.uk
www.celebrationoffood.co.uk
www.foodanddrinkfestival.com

pages 82-83
Revel in Film
www.idfa.nl
www.poff.ee
www.lcff.co.uk
www.goldenhorse.org.tw
www.sundance.org
www.slamdance.com
www.clermont-filmfest.com
www.baf.org.uk
www.cinemagic.org.uk
www.docudays.com
A Fiery New Year
www.biggarbonfire.org.uk
Go to the Carnival
www.carnivalofvenice.com
www.carnaval.qc.ca

pages 86-87
Dig It Up
www.archeaeology.co.uk
Friendly, Furry Helpers
www.petsastherapy.org
Make a Difference
www.csv.org.uk
Online Resources
www.idealist.org
www.experiencecorps.co.uk
www.timebank.org.uk
www.do-it.org.uk

pages 88-89
Give a Green Weekend
www.edenproject.com
Keep Cyclists Safe
www.sustrans.org
Hug a Tree
www.forestry.gov.uk
Help Heritage
www.nationaltrust.org.uk
Teach English Around the World
www.weekendtefl.co.uk

pages 90-91
Get Wet, Do Good
www.reorafting.com
Help Save the World
www2.btcv.org.uk
¿Habla Ingles?
www.puebloingles.com
Assist Exotic Communities
www.gvi.co.uk
WWOOF Away!
www.wwoof.org
A Hand for Four-Legged Friends
www.sparealife.org
www.mossburn.org

pages 92-93
Ecotourism & Sustainable Travel
www.ecotourism.org

The Perils of Voluntourism
www.tourismconcern.org.uk/pdfs/kates.pdf

pages 94-95
Unforgettable Help
www.elephantsanctuary.org
Don't Desert the Desert
www.sunseed.org.uk
Twitcher's Paradise
www.rspb.org.uk
Helping Out in Africa
www.ikando.org
Lending a Hand in the Himalaya
www.vsnnepal.org
www.infonepal.org
www.handsforhelp.org.np
Empower Village Women
www.sacafound.org
www.vcxp.org

pages 96-97
Behold the Turtle
www.banyantree.com
www.watamuturtles.com
Get Acquainted with an Ass
www.thedonkeysanctuary.org.uk
Become a Good Samaritan
www.samaritans.org.uk
Clown Around
www.theodora.org
www.clowndoctors.co.uk

pages 100-101
Slow Motion
www.walking-routes.co.uk
www.go4awalk.com
www.sustrans.org.uk
Go Batty
Newark Park Bat Walk, Gloucestershire (tel 0870 3000579; booking required)
Bat Walk, Renishaw Hall, Derbyshire (tel 01246 432310; booking essential)
Bat Watch, Glenbranter Forest, Argyll Forest Park (tel 01369 860703; booking required)
Gather Nature's Bounty
www.thefoxhunter.com
Spot a Sea Mammal
www.seawatchfoundation.org.uk/event-marine.htm

pages 102-103
Dine in the Dark
www.danslenoir.com
As Slow as Melting Chocolate
www.ashburtoncookeryschool.co.uk
www.lenotre.fr

pages 104-105
More Than a Treasure Hunt
www.spacehijackers.co.uk/letterboxing
Barge Into Tranquillity
www.justcanals.co.uk
Bite by Leisurely Bite
www.slowfood.com

pages 106-107
Relaxation, Pure & Natural
www.chumbeisland.com
Why Fly When You Could…Hit the Rails
www.thetrainline.com
www.railchoice.co.uk
Why Fly When You Could…Take to the High Seas
members.aol.com/CruiseAZ/home.htm

pages 108-109
Challenge for Charity
www.plymouth-dakar.co.uk
Walk It
www.greatoceanwalk.com.au
Clip-Clop
www.irishhorsedrawncaravans.com

pages 112-113
Make 'em Laugh
improvland.com/links/greatbritain.html
At the Gee-Gees
www.britishhorseracing.com
Strum, Blow or Beat Something
www.highlandpiping.co.uk
www.thepipingcentre.co.uk
www.musicteachers.co.uk
Slave It Out
www.slavercise.com

pages 114-115
Buzz Off
www.bbka.org.uk
Tame the Wild Outdoors
www.uksurvivalschool.co.uk
For the Birds
www.thehawkingcentre.co.uk
www.impact-falconry.co.uk

pages 116-117
Get Your Hands Dirty
www.allotment.org.uk
www.allotments.com
Go Underground
www.darkplaces.co.uk
Do Your Own Adaptation
www.mckeestory.com
Tree-Top Hideaways
www.mighty-oak.co.uk
www.thetreehouseguide.com
Quirky Getaways
www.landmarktrust.org.uk

pages 118-119
Get Your Gear Off
www.british-naturism.org.uk
www.irishnaturism.org/index.php
Befriend the Big Five
www.gamecapture.info

pages 120-121
Get Stuffed! The Fall & Rise of Taxidermy
www.taxidermy.org.uk
www.taxidermists.co.uk
Dark Tourism
www.dark-tourism.org.uk

pages 122-123
Appreciate the Outsiders
www.outsiderart.co.uk
Learn to Sign
www.british-sign.co.uk
Go Eco
www.cat.org.uk
Up In Lights
www.bbc.co.uk/jobs/workexperience/index.shtml
www.nyfa.com
www.aaft.com
www.brightonfilmschool.org.uk
www.britfilms.com
www.screentrainingireland.ie

credits

Amelia Thomas
A British writer and journalist working between the UK, Israel and the Palestinian Territories, Amelia was formerly a features journalist in Amsterdam, where she covered Russian clowns, Dutch dominatrixes, Nigerian scam artists, laughter-yoga teachers and an artist who married herself. She's lately been spending time with Egyptian camel drivers, sleeping up high in Turkish tree houses, sampling the restaurants of the Gaza Strip for Lonely Planet and experiencing a wealth of great British days out with her three-year-old, two-year-old and newborn baby. Amelia and her husband recently bought a tumbledown cottage high in the mountains of southern Bulgaria, which they're about to begin renovating, and her favourite places in the world are Shimla, Ambleside, Bethlehem, Cairo and Boulder, Colorado.

Author thanks
Big thank yous to the friends and family who've offered advice, suggestions and knowledge on what they do – or would like to do – in their free time, and for their unflagging support: Fran Thomas, Ellen Pearce, Amy Robertson, Kamal Chaoui, Judith Sudilovsky, Yoran Bar and lots of others. Thanks too to my fantastic editor, Stefanie Di Trocchio, for being communicative, understanding, and generally wonderful, to Travis Drever for his fabulous design work, and to the many others at Lonely Planet for making 132 come together. Finally, thanks, as ever, to Gal for always being there.

Behind the Scenes
Commissioning Editor: Stefanie Di Trocchio
Publishing Manager: Imogen Hall
Designer: Travis Drever
Proofer: Janine Eberle
Product concept: Laetitia Clapton

The Free-Time Continuum chapter was written by Kitty Melrose based on text provided by Amelia Thomas.

Special thanks go to Roz Hopkins, Annika Roojun, Clifton Wilkinson, Fayette Fox, Jennifer Bilos, Katrina Marks, Liz Lindsay, Richard Samson and Stephen Palmer.

Thanks also to Amanda Canning, Bridget Blair, Briony Grogan, Fiona Buchan, Fiona Siseman, Jane Pennells, Malcolm O'Brien, Nic Lehman, Paula Hardy, Robin Goldberg, Sally Schafer and Tom Hall.

1

132

go ahead. seize the days.